MW01227612

We Should All Be Rich Friends

Your Ultimate Circle of Success

Dr. Tasha McCray

Forward by Myron Golden, Ph.D.

We Should All Be Rich Friends

Copyright © 2023 by Dr. Tasha McCray

All rights reserved. No part of this book may be reproduced or transmitted in any form or by any means without written permission of the author.

ISBN 979-8854236140

Forward

Dr. Tasha McCray's "We Should All Be Rich Friends" is so powerful and so very different than you might think from the title. Even though I have known Dr. McCray for several years, I was still blown away by this book. It took me less than a week to read and I must say I was impacted more than impressed and I was really impressed.

Proverbs 13:20 says, He that walketh with wise men shall be wise: But a companion of fools shall be destroyed. That is what I believe the essence of this book is about.

It has been said that your net worth will be plus or minus the average of our 5 closest friends. We should all be rich friends because it is the pleasant, profitable, and practical thing to do. If you don't have any rich friends, you drastically reduce your chances of becoming a rich friend. As iron sharpens iron, so does a person sharpen the countenance of their friends.

I have spent most of my career seeking to assist people in understanding how to create and cultivate a fortune so they can set their families free. I believe this book encapsulates the principles necessary for anyone who is serious about getting rich.

As you read "We Should All Be Rich Friends" don't just write down what Dr. McCray says in the book, write down what you think of as a result of what she says in the book.

The good news is, if you follow the advice and instructions given in this book, you will find yourself as a rich person surrounded by your rich friends. I hope that I get to be one of them.

Myron Golden, Ph.D.

Acknowledgements

Acknowledging the Incredible Reader's Round Table!

I am deeply grateful for the unwavering support and dedication of the following amazing individuals who formed the Reader's Round Table for this book release:

Katina D.
Cherese P.
Diana D.
Tenisha C.
Dr. Catrina S.
Tina P.
Dr. Tonya B.
Dr. Anshanette T.
Yvette D.

These extraordinary ladies have played an integral role in bringing this book to life. Their invaluable feedback, encouragement, and enthusiasm have made this journey even more rewarding and meaningful.

To each member of the Reader's Round Table, I extend my heartfelt appreciation for your time, insights, and belief in the power of this book's message. Your contributions have undoubtedly enriched this project, and I am honored to have shared this experience with you.

Thank you for being a part of this empowering journey, and for being shining examples of women supporting women. Together, we are making a difference, and I am excited to continue this transformative path with each one of you.

With utmost gratitude,

Dr. T Mac

Introduction

Dear Rich Friend,

This book was crafted with YOU in mind—the one who deserves a life of true richness in every sense. Not just in finances, but in every beautiful aspect that makes life extraordinary: ideas that spark brilliance, connections that ignite our spirits, imagination that knows no bounds, relationships that nurture our souls, results that leave a mark, and a community that uplifts and supports.

My deepest desire is for you to live abundantly, with no regrets holding you back! Together, let's embark on a journey of empowerment, growth, and fulfillment. Let's be "Rich Friends" who inspire each other to achieve greatness and embrace the joyous abundance life has to offer.

Are you ready to unlock the limitless possibilities within you? Then let's start this transformative adventure together!

With love and excitement,

Dr. T Mac

Table of Contents

1 Be Rich In Ideas

We should all be rich friends. Why do I say that?

Well first you should be rich. Secondly, it only makes sense that your friends should be rich too. Why should your friends be rich? I'm glad you asked. This is a question of environment. You are who you surround yourself with, and your connections become a reflective picture of your future. How you connect and to whom you connect yourself with becomes a driving force, first, to how you see yourself, and secondly, towards what you eventually become.

If you desire to be rich, it all must start with a vision. When most people consider the term rich, money comes to mind. But in truth, money is only a reflection of a great imagination. One of my mentors taught me that when it comes to imagination, imagination is the foundation for optimal success. Never discount the things that come to your mind that lend itself towards your own greatness. Riches follow vision, moreover, riches follow an extreme and ingenious imagination. Imagination is a human gift and a gift granted to human beings exclusively. You are free to imagine your future in whatever terms you desire, and when it comes to imagination, there is absolutely no limit to the imagination.

Before I share my story, I will share with you the acronym that I developed for the term Rich Friends. They are as follows.

Resourceful

Influential

Collaborative

Helpful

Fearless

Resilient

Innovative

Empathetic

Nurturing

Determined

Supportive

I will pull from these terms throughout this book in no particular order. But these are the elements that comprise the recipe for accomplishment. Being wealthy or rich has a beginning. All of life is based on how you start, and how you start is based off of what you see in yourself and then what you can see beyond yourself that is a reflection of what you value. It is the quality of this sight, or better stated, it is the quality of insight that determines your future. In addition to the acronym of rich friends, I will provide you with five keys to an optimal beginning towards your highest intention according to what you want in life.

1. You must understand who you are. Rich in Personal Value.
2. You must clearly know what you desire. Rich in What You Want.
3. You must have a distinct knowledge system. Rich in Knowledge.
4. You must be innovative. Rich in Ideas.
5. You must be extremely and exclusively determined. Rich in Where You Are Going.

Nothing should distract you from these five keys. These five keys are non-negotiable, and they must be at the forefront of your consciousness at all times. You cannot let your environment impact what you envision. No matter the circumstances there must remain an extreme focus on the intention that you have set for yourself. Life cannot interrupt your potential. Allow me to share my story with you.

At the age of 13, I got pregnant. My mom had me at 16 and was a single parent. Life was rough then, so the trajectory of my future as a 13-

year-old pregnant girl was grim to say the least. I had heard it all. From the time I got pregnant to the day I delivered; I heard every day that I would never amount to anything. You're just going to be one of those girls. You're going to have 5 or 6 baby daddys. You're going to be on welfare your whole life. I heard all these things while I was pregnant at thirteen.

When my son turned 5 months old, I was kicked out of the house. It was the same night, when I went to my grandma's, my grandma said, "Let's pray". We got and our knees to pray and my grandma started praying for my mom. My grandmother started thanking God for allowing her to come get us and to take care of us. Then my grandma looked at me and said, "You can be, do, and have anything you desire".

At 14 years old, that was my first time ever hearing "Be, Do, Have". This comes from my mentor who uses the story in the book of Genesis in the Bible that explains our personal power. **Be** fruitful, **Do** multiply, and **Have** dominion. I had borrowed my grandmother's belief, when then, even at that age, it became a driving force in my life. I knew then that my life wasn't over, contrary to what my mom had to say. My life wasn't over. She instilled that in me. My mom had me quit school, but with this newfound knowledge of my greatness, I got back in school.

I got back on the cheerleading team. I then graduated at 17. Became a nurse at 18. Opened a hair salon at 20. I was now an entrepreneur. I did all the things my grandmother told me I could do. There was a defined space of tragedy that awaited me based on the statistics of young women my age and color. My mother was affirming that in my life. It was my grandmother through a language that was more consistent to the greatness and potential in me, that spoke life instead of death. I did have a choice to who I would listen to. I chose to hear and adopt and adapt what my grandmother spoke into me. It was a defining moment for me. My journey to an extraordinary life had begun.

You too are guaranteed an extraordinary life. But this life is hinged on how you start. It is hinged on how you view your own future, and then act within the space of your "beginnings". Being rich along with having rich friends is a vital life force. It is an energy. Some will choose to live outside of their potential, and that's ok. But it is always a choice. I had two different voices in my ear, but I chose the values that my grandmother shared with me.

This led me to create a rich friends circle. Why must we all be rich friends? This is a premium way to make sure that the correct values are spoken around you. It is easy for a person to speak their tragedy into your life. These spoken values are extremely definitive, and yes, they will define you well before you get the chance to define yourself.

Now let's take a closer look at these five keys to ensure you're off to a great start with your intentions.

1. You must understand who you are. Rich in Personal Value.
2. You must clearly know what you desire. Rich in What You Want.
3. You must have a distinct knowledge system. Rich in Knowledge.
4. You must be innovative. Rich in Ideas.
5. You must be extremely and exclusively determined. Rich in Where You Are Going.

Rich In Personal Value

You must understand who you are. This is a non-negotiable notion. Understanding who you are makes you rich in personal value.

What do I mean by personal value?

You'll be surprised as to how many people can value things but find it hard to assess value within themselves. Here's the shocker. You actually have no value until you define the value and then designate that value. Value is something that doesn't happen automatically because you're born into this world. Value is initially given to you by those who care and love you.

A mother feeds you and nurses you because she sees value in you, mainly because she gave birth to you. What is it that is seen in a child by her mother? What about a father who takes care of a child by providing for that child? Essentially, if you ponder the question long enough, you will come to the realization that value is assessed by what those parents see in that child as it pertains to their future. A parent, even before a child is born, has hopes and dreams for that child. Value is assessed based on what a person becomes in the world, but that value begins with how someone sees that person, moreover, acts towards that person based on what they see in that person. Value here is two-fold.

True value begins with a picture. Most people never realize that they don't take the time to develop a picture of their future. This is why the imagination is so powerful. But for many, their lives are defined for them, therefore leaving them in an extremely unhappy state of being. There are so many elements in life that can do the defining for you. It could be the environment that you were raised in. It could be parents that have their own ideology as to what you should be. It could be a schoolteacher. It could be a boss or a particular job that's defining your life. It could be a religion or a learned belief system that defines your life. Moreover, it could be circumstances or very specific experiences that end up defining who you are and where you're going. This also can be a relationship or an experience within that relationship that becomes defining. It can be a defining moment.

All of these are external agencies that can play a role at defining who you are. But when you take a closer look at how life really works, definition should come from within you. Again, this is the power of the imagination. Most people live lives that are defined for them, the truly happy live a life that's defined by themselves. There's a Bible scripture that says, that without a vision people perish. This is actually a biophysical fact. You are designed to dream dreams, and moreover, you are designed to accomplish those dreams. From a biophysical standpoint, your brain immediately communicates with your body when you set an intention for your future. Your body then immediately begins the process to calculate that dream in your adrenal gland. Your body then releases adrenaline that will drive you towards that dream.

This process alone proves the necessity of a recognized value within yourself as you develop it, or the necessity of designing a future for yourself outside of environmental influences and outside of environmental factors. Anything that's external should not define you. The entirety of your definition must come from you. This means you must be rich in ideas. You must be rich in your imagination. The beginning of all great things starts from within a person. It all starts from within you.

Every great invention came from within a person based on what they saw – a picture. Who you determine yourself to be becomes something in the world that others can experience and enjoy. Most of our greatest businesses that impact the world today, started in somebody's garage. Amazon, Apple Inc, Microsoft, Dell Computers, Walt Disney World, Google, Harley Davidson, etc. Someone had a vision within their mind and then valued that vision. In addition, they immediately began to work on that vision because of what they saw for the future.

Because my grandma saw value in me, this enabled me to correctly dream about what I can do in my own future. This became my mode of action. My behavior patterns. My actions followed my values. When something comes to your mind that is an expression of your own greatness, you must respect and value that imagination or idea. It is the actions that you take that stem from your own vision that will lead you to your highest point of accomplishment. You must be rich in ideas.

Rich in What You Want

When I say it all starts from within you, this is not an arbitrary motivational statement. This is not a philosophical statement that is said because it sounds good. "It all starts from within you" is a fact and nothing less. It has been researched and documented, even Sigmund Freud himself recognized the power that your body holds as it concerns your ability to imagine a future. It can be said that your body is the home of your consciousness. Science now knows that the body in its entirety is the mechanism in which you hold memory. All of your cells play an extreme role and how you remember something, because the cells within your body contain memory.

Your Physical Body Holds Power

There are specialized cells in your body called pyramidal cells. These are the cells that assist in holding memory of direction. This study was done in mice that showed the brain firing as the mice assessed a memorized direction. What do I mean by memorized direction? Just that, it is your ability to remember where to go based on being there before. What is specifically unique about human beings, is that we can assess direction that doesn't exist yet. Once again, this is the power of the imagination. In addition, this shows that you are biophysically designed to dream a dream, and your body will assess the direction to accomplish that dream.

Somehow in our society, being rich has been something to be frowned upon. Especially, when it comes to our religious institutions, there seems to be this notion that being rich is not a favorable thing to do, because it comes across as being selfish. But if you specifically look at the design of your body and how it works to optimize accomplishment, being rich is the default state of our human existence. Being poor or in poverty or having less than what you are valued at goes against nature. You are born to have more. This is a law that is built into the Earth. Be fruitful and multiply. There is nothing spiritual about not having what you deserve in life. You are designed to desire things. You must be rich in your desires.

All great things begin with a "wanting". Life itself as we know it began with God wanting it to be what it is. You are designed to want things so things can be. Life does not happen without wanting. Even as a child, sometimes we're told not to want things, especially if those things seem to be out of our reach. It is with this notion that we gain the feeling of being undeserving. This is the practice of poverty. You must change your understanding and know that wanting a decided future that you designed is extremely necessary.

Begin with writing things down. Here are some pointers.

A. You must always document what you want. What you document must be done with extreme clarity. Clarity will spawn an emotion. When you become real clear, it feels like an ah ha moment. A feeling is the movement of hormones within your body. When the hormones are released from a series of glands, you can then be assured that you are clear and certain on what you want.

B. You must be specific about what you want. Your body records everything and your memory works better accomplishing when there are specific details. What kind of car you want. What kind of house you want. How many bedrooms. The square footage. How big is the kitchen? Where and how do you travel. Is it first class or private? What business do you own? How much money are you making and how often. Your body's memory system deals in specifics.

C. What you desire in life must be compelling. Do not ever think small; or worse, do not think in terms of "just enough". Your body's nervous system reacts off of memory. If you are stuck in a cycle of things that you don't want, the memory of what you do want must be greater in order to impact your nerve cells. You must think big. You must think expensive. You must think expansive. If you value yourself, you must dream at the highest values.

D. Then you must constantly and consistently review what you want until you have it. Achieving what you desire in life helps others to see their own potential. Serving yourself with the highest good, becomes good for others.

Begin with knowing what these things are. Be rich in what you want. Be rich in what you desire in life.

Be Rich in Knowledge

Have a Knowledge System. What do I mean by that? Most people go with the old adage "You must believe in yourself", or simply, "You must believe". What does that really mean to believe? Some say it's a matter of faith or a strong conviction about something or someone. Some say it's a mind thing or a state of mind. Let me share a little secret… if you're believing in something, the natural implication is that what you "believe" is not there. People say, "you must believe in order to make it come to fruition, manifest, or make it happen". Again, I want to bring your body's magnificent ability to form memory.

Have you ever spent the energy of believing for something and it never happened?

Memory works with knowledge. Memory through the body is converted into action. This is the work of the cells within your nervous system. But when you believe, the natural energetic imprint is that in which you believe is not there. This is why you are told to "believe", because your focus is on the "not there". If that's what your cells memorize, then the "not there" is the only thing that the cells have to go on. Therefore, your body directs you mostly to the space of nothing. To resolve this matter, you must begin with what you know versus what you believe. Knowledge becomes an actual stored memory; therefore, your body responds directly to knowledge.

Belief invokes effort. Knowledge invokes birth. As a matter of fact, under the notion of belief the "not there" becomes a satisfactory sensation, because your body is still processing something. It's just processing a "not there". Get out of the habit of saying, "I believe" and into the habit of saying, "I know". This makes a huge difference in the energy that's directed towards results and achievement.

Here's where it gets really exciting. There's knowledge that comes from learning and then there's knowledge that comes from seeing. The knowledge that stems from learning can come from educational institutions, what your parents might teach you, the experiences that you have, your religion, and so on. But you must know this beyond knowing, the most important knowledge stems from your imagination in the form of ideas. This means you must convert from believing that you can accomplish a myriad of your desires, to knowing that you will accomplish anything that comes to your imagination.

Use the more powerful adage, Knowledge is Power.

Here's the key. You can decide what you know. Formulate a System of Knowledge that works on your behalf. How is this done?

Your "system of knowledge" must be tied directly into what you want and what you desire for your life. This is why it is of the upmost importance that you are clear on what you want. It must ring with clarity. This is the first energy of knowledge. Let's list out the others.

1. Knowledge begins with crystal clarity. A crystals color signifies that all impurities has been removed from the crystal. You must be clear about your vision. Other "stuff" cannot be mixed in.
2. Then there's the knowledge you decide to associate with. This comes through the Language towards you.

You want to make sure that those who are around you possess the capacity to speak the equivalent language of your dreams, and then carry the content of who you are and what you desire within them. This creates a more accurate dialog according to your vision. When this body of personages have in addition, an expertise or training in the area of what you want, they can consistently offer new knowledge as it concerns what you want.

You want to converse or have conversations in places where you are learning more about the mechanisms of your destiny. Think about how many conversations you might have during the course of the day that has nothing to do with what you want or where you are going. These non-knowledge spaces are essentially costing you.

3. Then there are spaces of knowledge.

Put yourself in the spaces of knowledge that are consistent to your destination. When the hieroglyphics were discovered in Egypt, it was initially assumed that the Egyptians were 97% illiterate, because the archeologists could not decipher the text. Wow. They couldn't read it, so

I guess the culture couldn't read either. It was later determined that it was the exact opposite. 97% of the Egyptian population was highly literate. This is because "book knowledge" wasn't the crowning point of education. Hieroglyphics were literally everywhere on the walls, the floors, the temple, the pillars of the buildings, etc. Because of this, it invoked an understanding, even in the babies, because that's all they saw all day every day.

When you move in the spaces of places that are consistent with your dream, you are then constantly gaining knowledge, which is immediately converted into memory. Oprah Winfrey says that your house or home must give rise to who you are. With this, you can take advantage of the space on your walls to hang pictures that contain elements of your vision. Statues and knick-knacks in your home can reflect directly on where you are going. You can even have the music that fills your environment to speak to your destination. Design your home to reflect the knowledge needed to accomplish your vision.

And then, of course, read books, listen to books, attend seminars, events, and weekend workshops that contain the necessary knowledge. These are all good, but the best thing you can do to enhance the space of your knowledge, is to be a part of a community that contains living examples of the pictures you have drafted for your future. A lot of people believe that they can accomplish their desire, but then do none of this.

You must be rich in knowledge.

Be Rich in Ideas

What you imagine, although not in physical existence yet, is also a form of knowledge. As a matter of fact, it is the premier form of knowledge. You should always value what you imagine, and you must always value your ideas. Knowledge that doesn't exist so to speak, always comes into existence through the space of someone's imagination. To be sure, the space of your imagination is the beginning of knowledge.

Every idea that serves mankind, especially when it comes to the improvement and the betterment of mankind, has an associated value. This is the basis of riches and wealth. Ideas are immediate knowledge. I consider ideas to be privileged knowledge. Your body goes to immediate work to culminate your idea into physical knowledge so it can be turned into useful action. An idea becomes no good if action does not ensue. The value inside of you as it concerns your idea, must be converted to a value outside of you. That's the purpose of an idea. It is the culmination of that idea into an experience for you and others.

Your Idea = Knowledge = Value

For the most part, that idea will turn into a form of business and space of trade, wherein you can and will build riches and wealth. Working for time or trading your time for money will limit your ability to gain perpetual riches. Moreover, in that space you are typically getting paid to bring someone else's idea into fruition. It is the imagination that affords you the opportunity to gain an unlimited source of perpetual riches. A rich life begins with being rich in ideas.

Now everyone is gifted with the ability to formulate ideas, but you must give yourself the space for those ideas to come, much by using the technology of gaining knowledge. You must put yourself in an environment that creates the state for ideas to flow. A good place to start is to hang around people who are specialists at formulating ideas and then make those ideas happen. With this, you are associating yourself with the energy of creation.

Your Idea = Creation

Conversion

Make this word a part of your regular vocabulary. Conversion. Creation is a series of conversions. Life is about conversion. Everything in terms of nature has a beginning, then converts from that beginning state to a final state within a series of stages. This is the natural flow of life. Conversion. When you have an idea, you are usually picturing the finished state of that idea. This is sufficient for your body to store that idea as a memory within your cells.

Here is what's special about the human body. The initial stages of conversions happen directly in your body. This is where you begin to feel the energy of your idea well up in your body. This is because your idea is so compelling that it moves the energy within your body. This energy that you feel is literally the hormones flowing from your glands as a result of your idea. You are feeling the conversion.

What this does is force the revelation of what is necessary to accomplish the idea that came from you. It's amazing how your body plays an intricate role when it comes to accomplishment. Now it's up to you to further convert that idea into what you will physically see. When you think of the foremost leading corporations in the world, both in establishing something new, and then the wealth associated with it, you are looking at what was once an idea in a single person's head. All ideas are meant to convert. Here's a short strategy for ideas and imagination.

1. Immediately write out anything you envision, any idea, any notion that comes to you.
2. Pay close attention to how you feel.
3. Immediately out of those feelings will come the strategy for accomplishment. Be sure to write down everything you can as it comes to your mind.
4. Next, build teams around your idea. These must be relationships of competency. Build relationships in accordance with where you are going. Your destination.

Rich in Where You are Going

Being rich in where you are going is a matter of determination. When you think of the word determination you must think of the word focus. For every idea there is a finishing point stemming from that idea. Life converts your idea until it reaches a finishing point. Another characteristic of a finishing point that launches from an idea is that the finishing point should be perpetual. Allow me to explain.

When Steve Jobs went into what is considered a wilderness experience, he envisioned the desktop computer. When he returned, the idea was an energetic presence within him, so much so, his work, moreover, his actions towards his idea happened immediately. Like my grandmother, it was Steve Jobs' father who invested into him his sense of value towards his future. This investment is always vital to the strength of your idea. It is for this reason that you keep yourself around competent relationships. Keep people around you that can see your value and act towards your value.

Once Steve Jobs accomplished his first prototype and then his first line of production, it was this invention that launched a series of ideas, which in perpetuity, Apple Inc became the first US company to reach a trillion dollars in valuation. Apple Inc became the influence in how we listen to our music and revolutionized the cell phone. Not only did Steve Jobs reach the space of his vision, but many other visions were launched from there. At its core, this took sheer determination.

Let's take a closer look at determination. When I had the idea to become a beautician and open my own shop, because I was so young, it took pure determination. But my grandmother had invested in me her vision of me. I carried that energy throughout the process. The root word of determination is termination or terminal.

Every idea and vision has a termination point. Determination is your ability to stay focused on the terminal point. This is the exact same process that takes place when you fly. When you board a flight and then take off, you fly directly into a specific terminal at an airport. Here's what's important. Once a destination is set, everything on that airplane is geared to reach that terminal. When you look at the instruments on the jet's panel, there are so many gauges for measurement. The main panel measures in degrees. If you were flying from New York to Los Angeles, and you were just a half of degree off, you will never make it to Los Angeles.

Every idea has a terminal point. Like those jet instruments, everything you do from the inception of your idea must be geared towards your terminal point. Otherwise, you will never reach your destination. The riches in the space of your destinations are the accurate actions that you take to reach your destination.

Your idea and the destination of your idea are two equal parts of the same thing. Your idea as an idea is a clear picture of your destination. As your idea appears, so does your destination simultaneously appear. The space between the two is where your riches lie. You must be rich in the actions that you take within that space. That space is like an airplane cockpit. Everything must be consistent and geared towards the destination. Ideas flourish among actions that are consistent with your ideas. Your actions must be focused. Your focus is paramount to your terminal, which is the essence of determination.

Your determination has to be calculated out as you move forward towards your destination. Every move you make has a value associated with your idea. As you learn these actions from what comes to mind or learn them from your mentors, document the necessary movements and take action. Be consistent.

The Road to Your Rich Space and Friends

You now have some tools that will assist you in creating the life you want or desire. It all begins with your personal value. This value is directly associated with sight. Moreover, insight. How do you see yourself? The next major question is, how do others see you? When I was pregnant at thirteen, my mother had the worst things to say about me. She only spoke into me what she believed. She could only believe what she had seen in her own life. And I am sure, these beliefs were spoken into her, and that became her value system. But my grandmother spoke into me what she knew. Knowledge trumps belief any day.

I took the information that was consistent towards my greatest future and went with that knowledge. That became my compass similar to that which is found on an airplane. My focus was locked in, and I designed the space of my future. I used my ideas to create a compelling future. Now you can and must, using the components of success, use your own imagination to create a map of the greatest future possible for your life. You too can, from any circumstance or situation, use your imagination to draft out anything you desire. Your idea can cast you far beyond any place that you are currently experiencing.

Nothing in life is a final point, because your imagination can immediately exist in a different space and place. The key is to make your idea or imagination a point of knowledge. Your body will then work with you to solidify what you want. In order for your idea to convert into the experience of what you want, you must take consistent actions towards what you want. In addition to these actions, place yourself in environments that accord to what you want. Most importantly, create competent relationships that accord to your direction. It is then that you will experience the riches both in yourself and with your friends.

2 Be Rich In Connections

If I was to ask you the question, what do you want, what would your answer be? This is a question that most people never really put any thought into. Another thing that most people do not realize is that wanting is central to having vision, which is a necessary part of life. What do I mean?

Clarity is the key to making things happen. You must begin the journey of your intentions with clarity. You must be clear about what you want in life. As far as your intention is concerned, it all begins with the all-important question, what do you want? What is your desire for your life? This is a space that needs to be designed and then defined. There must be a want. There must be a desire. These wants come in the form of pictures, which is essentially vision.

Think of vision as an energy. When you have a vision, this energy works on your behalf because it is energy. Energy stays in a state of motion and when you have a vision, those pictures that you hold within are constantly in motion. Everything that you determine for your future is immediately set in motion. Here's the key to accomplishment and the key to getting the things you want in life. You must stay in the space of the motion that's already in movement on your behalf.

The human gift is that humans have a uniqueness to their consciousness. You and I have the ability to paint pictures beyond the space of any obstacle, circumstance, or situation that may seem to hinder your progression. When you design and define a future vision or set an intention for your life, that vision based on its movement or natural motion remains beyond any present circumstance. The reason you can feel stuck at times is based on when you move yourself out of the space of your own greatness.

How do you maintain that space?

The answer.

Your relationships.

As I mentioned earlier, it was my grandma that had a knowledge of me that I did not have about myself. Being born in a line of tragedy and trauma, my mom's handling of my situation as a young 13-year-old was abusive to say the least. The language towards me could have defined me. But when she put me out, the blessing was that it gave my grandma the opportunity to take care of me. This set in my life a different trajectory.

When you think of forming your relationships, you must form your relationship with those that will put your life on the best trajectory possible. This is a measurable fact, or at least it should be. When it comes to your relationships, you must begin to take measurement. When it came to all of my early relationship with men, this was not the case. When it comes to relationships, you must recognize that your relationships have the greatest impact on your progression.

The Relationship Drama

Allow me to share with you a couple of short stories from my previous book "WHERE IS MY LIFE PARTNER?: A WOMAN'S GUIDE TO ATTRACTING HER SOUL MATE. I had a conversation with a friend of mine, and her name was Karen. She was highly concerned about not finding that life partner to share her life with. She was extremely frustrated. I asked her the question, "what is it costing her by not solving this problem? She stated, "Not finding that person who I can spend the rest of my life with is costing me peace and happiness and a healthy body." She needed that relationship.

I was in an ongoing series of relationships, but it's amazing how you might think you have filled that space, but you don't calculate what you are filling that space with. A cost is always associated with a connection.

A Cost Is Always Associated with A Connection.

1

At the age of nineteen, I married a man who I grew up with, he was only one year older than myself. I knew his family, we shared the same friends, and came from the same town. I had my life planned out with this person who was going to be my forever love regardless of our young ages. Everything was going well between us for about one month, then all hell broke loose. He lost his job, stop paying his part of the bills, and was not in search for employment. At the time, I thought that maybe he was going through some type of depression that would be short lived. After about three months of no support from him, I knew that we were in trouble.

Without giving all the details, my husband wasn't really interested in being a provider. Over the span of five months, we lost our family car, our electricity was disconnected for a short while, bills got behind, and we almost lost our home. We received some assistance from family, but that got old as their resources were very limited. I was lost, broke, and had no clue of which direction to take in our new marriage that was already full of despair and confusion.

Trying to hold onto what little faith I had was a daily challenge for me. I prayed day and night for help and guidance. I went to church every time the doors were open seeking answers. One day after bible study, I received counsel from an old church friend who told me not to look for employment that my husband was supposed to provide. This was definitely not the answer I was looking for. It did not make sense to me as we were extremely behind in bills with no chance of catching up if I could not work to contribute. All of my attention was on raising my children and paying bills. The marriage was certainly not a priority…I was in survival mode!

Six years had quickly passed, and I knew that the marriage was over. Rumors of infidelity and drug abuse by my husband took a toll on my sanity. There were many days and nights where I had visions of what my future looked like, and it scared the hell out of me. I could not take it anymore, so I packed up my children and left. We moved into a small apartment and started over, alone. It was not easy, but at least we were in a better position, and I was hopeful that better days were ahead.

Six years! Wow!

2

I had a month-long courtship with a guy, let's call him Will. Well, Will and I had grown very fond of each other during our short-lived relationship. He showered me with gifts, time, and affection just before sitting me down to dinner to inform me of his wedding that was to occur in one week. What?! A wedding?! What do you mean by wedding? I was totally confused. I mean, how can you date me steadily and be engaged to someone else? Let me tell you...I still haven't gotten a straight answer. I don't think that I need to tell you what happened there. Boy, bye!

Even though I never spoke to him again, I was devastated. How could I be so gullible? How could I not see the signs of another woman? We had barely gotten started and I had already fallen for this guy. I was utterly embarrassed. I had left a bad marriage just to end up with someone who cared nothing about my feelings.

3

Once I finished nursing school, I packed up my children and moved to Florida. Why Florida? To this day I have no definite answer. All I knew was that I closed my eyes and pointed to a place on the map. We started our lives over and I was super excited because I had my independence, great career, and a fresh beginning at discovering new things. Well, to be honest, I didn't start completely over. My boyfriend at the time helped move us to Florida. Yes, you read that right…another boyfriend. Anyway, he wasn't too thrilled about it since I did not include him, but I did make him an offer. He was not ready for the move. So, after he helped us unpack, he stayed a few days then left. He did visit once, but still no signs of wanting to live in Florida. We spoke a few times on the phone then he disappeared. A few months later, I got word that he had gotten married to his college sweetheart. Another one bites the dust.

4

After a year and a half of being without a boyfriend, I was open to dating again. It so happened that a pharmacist who I worked with had the perfect guy in mind. She introduced us, we went out on a few dates, and of course, he wined and dined with me for about four months. Then he popped the big question. I said yes. We had a "secret" ceremony on a private island, honeymooned on another island, and started planning for our "big" wedding.

Less than one month into our union, he became emotionally abusive to me in private. He would pour cold water on me while I was sleeping, run me off the road while I was taking my kids to school or going to work, play mind games with me, and any other bad emotional thing he could think of at the time. I suffered in silence for a few months before I shared my experience with some of my family and friends. No one believed me! They would say things like, "He is too good to you. Are you sure? I can't believe that. You're just exaggerating." I promise that I was telling the truth, but I could not prove it because he wasn't physically abusive, and he always put on a good act in front of everyone.

But one night everything hit the fan. I had returned from working late at the hospital when he accused me of having an affair. He ripped my clothes off, pushed me on the bed and began to punch me in my stomach. He whispered in my ear, "I am hitting you here because you won't bruise on your stomach." I went into fight or flight mode instantly. I began fighting back with everything I had in me. We woke up the family with the sounds of our hustle and tussle. Everyone came to my rescue, I called the police, but he had left before they arrived.

All I could think about at that time was getting him as far away from me and my children as possible. I immediately filed a restraining order against him, sought a lawyer, and never spoke to him again until I had to face him in court. He had written a thirteen-page letter to the courts stating how I tried to kill him. The judge did not buy his story for several reasons, but mainly because I had a great attorney. But none of that mattered because once again, I was left with feelings of embarrassment, brokenness, and emotionally scattered.

5

My attorney, Fred, reached out to "check" on me several times while in my vulnerable, weakened, horrified state. We had long conversations about how I needed to be protected from that monster and how he could help me. And I am sure you already know what happened next. Yep, he helped me alright. We ended up dating. Are you seeing the pattern yet?

Fred and I dated consistently for one year. We split time between our homes as I refused to sell my home despite his constant urging. During the course of our relationship, I was treated like a queen. He took me and the children on wonderful vacations and all expenses were paid including my monthly bills. We were living the life. I had finally found the one who could make all my dreams come true. Life was great in my world.

Fred was a high-profile attorney who liked to show his appreciation to the judges and other high-profile professionals in his arena. Every year around Christmas he would have an extravaganza at his office complex. The city's who's who would be in attendance. This would be my first and last time being a part of his circus (but I did not know that at the time). He had flown me to several major cities in search of the most elegant dress for the main event. Fred had also flown in my auntie to share this occasion. Little did I know that every woman past and present would share the same space as I. All eyes were on me alright, but for the wrong reason. As soon as I showed up, I was met at the door by one of his mistresses who thought it important to inform me of her status as well as the other six or seven of his women.

I think you can figure out what happened next. Yes, you guessed it. Emotions were extremely high, and I was not going to be disrespected that night. I threw the worst temper tantrum ever. Informed the guest that I had invited of what was going on and threatened to leave the party. Taking the advice of my guest, I stayed, but I was not a happy woman, and everyone knew it. As soon as the party was over, so was I.

The next day I packed my bags and returned to my house lonely, embarrassed, and broken. I was determined that this would never happen to me again. I was completely done with men. I knew that something had to change and that it began with me. So, I started on my quest to heal and find peace with the common denominator, ME.

A Better Way

This pattern had to be interrupted. Here's where the interruption takes place, in addition, what it is that has to interrupt this pattern. ME!

What am I saying here? You must find value in who you are and that will assist you in the energy of how you select a partner. I'm here to assist you in not taking the same number of years to learn this valuable lesson. You must seek you first, and all the things that you desire in your life will be added. This is why the information I shared with you in the first chapter is critical. You must have clarity in your future design, because you will use that to measure how you connect with other people.

Clarity Leads to Competent Connections

If you do not take the time to reach this space of clarity, you will continue to connect with people who can't see your value, because you did not take the time to establish that value. This is where you break the pattern of relationships that in the end, waste your time. You must understand that relationship is about growth, and if you are not growing, you are in the wrong relationship. You cannot be afraid of this fact. Most people are terrified at moving out of a relationship that does not serve their greatest end. Most people are afraid of moving out of a relationship that does not serve their intention. You must first set an intention for your life, and then secondly, require whoever you are with to serve that intention.

I will share with you now a strategy based on "Love Me" that will assist you in the space of garnering relationships that will take you higher. Here it is.

L- Learn to listen to yourself.
O- Observe inner-feelings and own it.
V- Value/Validate feelings.
E- Evaluate your views.

M- Makeover (inner and outer).
E- Evolution.

Learn To Listen to Yourself

OK people. This is the secret of secrets. We all have had the following feeling our notion. Have you ever had the feeling that when something went horribly wrong based on a decision that you made, you say to yourself, "I knew that would happen"? We all have done it, and we have all had the revelation that you knew exactly what was going to go wrong when you make the decision to connect with a person, spend that money somewhere where it wasn't profitable, go to that place that caused you pain, etc. Again, we have all done it, but what's fascinating is that we knew in the beginning what was going to happen in the end, but we moved forward anyway.

When you get that inkling that a wrong decision is about to be made, why do we move forward anyway?

I'm glad you asked that question. We move forward anyway because we take our imagination and repaint the potential tragedy that's standing right in front of us. This is the misuse of your powerful imagination. This is literally a misplacement of your imagination. Your imagination is designed to construct your future, it is not designed to construct your relationship.

Your Imagination Is Designed to Construct Your Future, It Is Not Designed to Construct Your Relationship.

When you use your imagination to construct your relationship, your imagination is misplaced, because a relationship should not be constructed. A true relationship should be based on a person's ability to see who you are based on your intentions for your life. When you have clarity of intention that is a road map to your defined future, then a person who has the potential to connect with you must register that define future within them, and subsequently their behavior towards you must follow that line of sight.

What we do when we generally meet a person that has the potential of being a life partner, when these missing elements are read in the beginning by your intuition, we are well aware of what's missing. But we take and we imagine what things could be in the face of things being wrong. You simply take what is wrong and reimagine possibility. The key is, is that you cannot imagine another person's behavior pattern. That's why I said your imagination in this case is misplaced. When a person presents to you their flaws, which can be read immediately, you cannot negate those flaws in your mind and then redesign a different picture of potential.

Why?

Because when a person presents to you anything that's not who you are, or anything that's not moving in the direction of where you're going, that's active disrespect. What we do, is put up with the disrespect, and then hope for something different. Because you accepted this diminished presentation, then the individual you are connecting with has no reason to change. That's why from that point, things literally get worse. You don't even need to have a crystal ball to know that things are going to get worse. You literally know that from the beginning.

This is why I say, when you hear yourself telling you you're making the wrong decision or the wrong move, you must learn to listen to yourself versus moving forward with what is not going to work. This takes understanding your value and knowing the difference when that value does not show up in the other person.

I talked earlier about the body and how it works. Your body is truly the home of your subconscious based on how hormones move from gland to gland. This is how you register feelings within your body. Scientists have discovered that by the time you have a thought, that thought has existed biophysically in your body for seven seconds. Your body is so intelligent that it will tell you immediately that a connection in front of you is not good for you. That thought is then delivered, and then we are left with the choice to go with what we know or sit there and imagine something different. This imagination of what a relationship could be is a destructive imagination because that person should already be that when they meet you.

Why?

You can rest assured that when they meet you, their body is telling them how great you are, their body is telling them the needs that you have, their body is telling them how they can invest into you to make you greater. This is immediately read in their body. If there are any actions different from that accurate portrayal of you that they see immediately, it is because they choose to be different from what they know about you. This simply means, everything that comes after that is by choice and will be extremely damaging to your future and the intention that you have set for your future. If you have not set an intention for your future, then it doesn't matter. Just get ready for ongoing abuse, even if it's subtle.

When you hear that voice, "this is not going to work", that's the sound that you should base your action off of. If you reimagine what you know versus trusting yourself, you have constructed that damaging energy. Trust that early voice, which is your voice. Be rich in listening to yourself.

Observe Inner-Feelings and Own It

This is an extremely powerful notion. Pay attention to how you feel, because how you feel in the very moment is what's telling you the truth.

How you feel is not a mental reality nor is it a mind reality, how you feel is a biophysical reality. It's a system of chemicals that are running through your body that's projecting a message to your brain. Allow me to share with you what's happening when a person meets you and you feel that there is a potential connection.

First, your body we'll read the truth of that person's intention. Secondly, their body will read the truth of who you are. This is a biophysical fact. This is a biophysical system of communication based on pheromones, which are hormones released from both bodies. This communication happens without talk. This biophysical communication can read individual content within another person 100ft away or more, well before anyone of you say a word to each other. If you have an intention set for your future, that intention is built in your body, and when somebody meets you, their body will immediately read the intention of your greatness.

What happens from that point, if they are threatened by your presence, your capacity to do great things, your potential, and the like, it is because they read all of that up on meeting you. Sometimes, to be who they are, they will feel the need to reduce who you are. That's when they will deny your greatness and consciously plan to be a subtle adversary towards who you are and your intention for your future. This goes for both male and female. Trust me, in any type of relationship, they see who you are, but they have to deny it so they can feel that they are somebody.

You must learn to feel this when this is happening. Your body naturally knows the difference and will start to tell you that right away. Your body will speak directly to you. This is why it's important to establish within you a future plan, so much so, that your future plan gives you a feeling. When you walk around with the feeling that comes from your imagination or what you envision for yourself, you will more quickly pick up on when you're failing experiences are downturn at the presentation of somebody else. Be rich and how you feel and prioritize at all times those feelings.

Value and Validate

Value the intention that you set for yourself, then validate your future intention by measuring how people respond to that value. Because a person's body has the capacity to read the entirety of the energy protocol that you set for your future, they are literally faced with the choice of how they're going to respond to your greatness. You validate your value through their responses.

When I got pregnant at the age of 13, it was an opportunity for my mother to validate my value by still seeing my greatness. It took my grandmother to establish greatness in me based on what she saw in me. My grandmother was a validating energy because she saw my value. But now as you read earlier, i did not require that in the men that I dated and married. Now I know, it was the greatness in me that became a threat to their own value. So, most of them became abusive to increase their own value by making the effort of decreasing my value.

Now that I've learned to value and then validate, I have been more intentional about how I relate and then how I connect to others. Especially when it comes to the subject of a life partner. Be rich in your ability to value your imagination and then validate it through your connections.

Elevate Your Views

Elevating your views is an opportunity. Most people's viewpoint is controlled by their environment. What I mean by environment is any circumstance or situation that shapes your thinking. This can even be what a person has to say to you or not say to you, if it is shaping how you think, it still qualifies as an environment towards you. The way that it should happen is that once you establish value within yourself based on your future intentions for your greatness, when you are faced with challenges, you have the opportunity to elevate your imagination beyond the challenges.

Elevate Your Imagination Beyond Challenges

This is the gift of the human imagination, the human imagination can confront any circumstance, and even though those circumstances might present themselves as fact, you can reimagine something greater than the challenge. You can then focus on what you imagine, and not focus on the challenge or the circumstances that you're facing. Life will honor your imagination before it honors the attention that you might give to a challenge. There's a respect that life has towards something that's new and next. Life is naturally drawn to new and next. For the most part, your challenges should force you to think in the space of new and next.

Learn to elevate your views when you have situations or circumstances that present something outside of where you're going. That's a challenge to elevate in the moment and know something different than what you're looking at. This is where you turn back to, in the moment, learn to listen to yourself. Trust in the information that you're generating that will move you past any circumstance, situation, or challenges that you might face. They are all an opportunity to go higher.

The best plan is to in the moment when you imagine something greater than your circumstance, is you need to write it down immediately. First, respect what it is that comes to mind. Secondly, make it a requirement that others respect it in addition. Your viewpoint has value, so every time you elevate how you see things, you create more value that not only serves you, but that value in you will serve others. Be rich in how you view things.

Makeover

Makeover it's also an opportunity. These are the actions that you take based on elevated thinking. These are actions that you take based on the value that you see in yourself. Your actions must match your vision. When your actions do not match your valued vision, then what you said as an intent to value is immediately devalued because you've moved or acted in a different direction. The opportunity here is found in the fact that your personal response system can not only make over the situation that you might face, but it also takes you into a personal makeover.

Establishing value in your viewpoint or how you view things, and then elevating those views at every given opportunity, is entirely something that happens within the context of your thinking. Now you must act on your thinking to makeover. It's like baking a cake, if you put the wrong ingredients in and it doesn't taste right, you're not left at the mercy of what happened. Make it over. Using the same example of the cake, if you left it in the oven for too long and you burnt the cake. You are not at the mercy of the burnt cake, take action and make it over.

The same goes for life challenges. Everything will not turn out the way you want, but the exciting news is you can take what's in front of you and make it over. Again, this is an opportunity. This opportunity starts with the strength of your imagination, and then take the opportunity to act on what you see that's better then what's in front of you. This is the opportunity for a makeover. Be rich in your ability to make things over.

Act On What You See
That's Better Than What's in Front of You!

Evolution

Here's what's exciting about life, everything evolves. This natural tendency to evolve has been in place for billions of years. What makes you special as a human being, the space of your ability to evolve is limitless. Evolution is a natural tendency built into the Earth. But it only happens when something has reached a state of completion. Hence, when something is not completed, there is no tendency for evolution.

Let's put this puzzle together, when you learn to listen to yourself, it is due to the personal observation that you make of yourself. In this observation you must be honest with yourself. This honesty will lead you to make the corrections when you do fail to listen to the optimal language that comes from your greatest intention that you set for yourself. Then you must value this space, and as you value the space of your intention, it is validated by how others see you in that space. If people don't witness and then act correctly towards what you value, it is the highest sign of disrespect make another move. Moreover, move out of that energy.

When it's wrong, stop and make it over. This is where honesty comes in. You have to be willing to be wrong when it doesn't feel right. Never leave yourself at the mercy of the wrong viewpoint of another person. Once you get this right, then you will naturally evolve to greater spaces.

Love Me is a simple formula that will enable you to now garner the right relationships. When these relationships, especially those that are in the space of a life partner, definitely in the space of someone you are intimate with, when those relationships are right, then you are set to grow in the space of your intention.

Never Leave Yourself at
The Mercy of The Wrong Viewpoint of Another Person.

Be rich in your relationships!

3 *Have a Rich Story*

I would love to start this chapter by being unequivocal in this point, all growth stems from your relationships. For billions of years of bio development, this is the state where things are born from a seed and then due to environmental investments, that seed converts into a result. This is essentially the definition of growth, being able to convert into a result. There's a starting point, and then there is a finishing point. The "in between" is your growth.

Let's look at some obvious points of growth when it comes to the subject of agriculture or just simply how plants and trees grow, and we will use that to pattern our personal growth. This is definitely one of the areas wherein you should be extremely rich. You should be rich in growth.

Let's observe a plant or a tree and its process of growth. You essentially have the following stages.

1. You have the seed.
2. You have the germination of that seed.
3. You have the nurturing of what has germinated.
4. This nurturing not only includes watering, but it includes pulling up weeds at times.
5. During the process of nurturing that plant or tree will grow until it bears fruit.

This bearing of fruit represents the end result. I do want to refer to this end result as the basis of purpose. When something grows to where it produces something useful, that production represents purpose. To restate this in a correct order, you must first have clarity of vision, secondly build your relationships around your vision, and as a result of that relationship you achieve your purpose.

Production = Establishment of Purpose

Growth leads to the accomplishment of purpose. This is why your purpose must be stated with clarity as this clarity of purpose establishes personal value. When you plant a seed, the intent of your purpose is stored within the seed. When you have an idea, that idea becomes the seed to what will eventually be.

Purpose = Seed

Germination is a natural process that extends from the seed. When it comes to a plant or a tree, there is no work that is put in for germination to take place, only water. When it comes to growing a perpetual future from the starting point of the seed, a lot of us put in work where water is needed. You must look at your own growth from within this exact same process, because the vegetation that we see on Earth is the prerequisite of the growth potential that exists in you now. Quite simply, you are meant to grow.

The next natural phase is nurturing. This is where relationship enters back into the picture. There was a study that was done in Germany that involved the language development in early childhood. The test was on newborns to measure the effect of nurturing on a baby. You had a test sample of newborns that only received a diaper, and they bottle without being held or touched. Then you had another sample of newborns that was fed and head diaper changes, but in addition, they were cuddled, held, touched and nurtured. The study had to be brought to an immediate halt, because the obvious became even more obvious. The babies that weren't held and touched began to die a few days after birth.

Nurturing is central to your growth. Just as a plant needs nurturing for its growth, you need nurturing for your growth. This nurturing must come from an outside individual, which qualifies a relationship as being absolutely necessary for growth. Death might not ensue like it did with the newborns, but the study in Germany proves that nurturing plays an acute role in the health and well-being of who you are and where you're going. As your dreams begin to launch from the seed of your purpose, that germinated existence needs acute attention. But with this comes a grave responsibility.

What do I mean by responsibility?

You must make sure that the closest individuals around you have the capacity to first see your purpose, and then secondly, they must immediately respond to your purpose by nurturing the beginning of your purpose. This cannot happen without relationship. A great relationship is what I consider to be the water that exists towards your purpose.

Growth Monitoring

You must monitor your personal growth. Here's what I mean by that. You have to pay attention to the grounds in which your growth is taking place. Much like a plant, if things are growing around your purpose that's different or indifferent to the direction that you're going, those existences will consistently disturb the growth of your purpose. In this case, I'm associating those potential disturbances and distractions as weeds. Those weeds must be eliminated. Anything that's not like who you are or where you're going are the weeds that circumvent your purpose and your intention. They must go! You must understand this, and this is a point that's non-negotiable. This is why I call nurturing a responsibility. A lot of times we will hope for the weeds to convert and change into something that will better fit your intentions, but you must know, weeds do not change.

That's like planting a bed of roses and within that bed of roses are a bunch of weeds. You come to water those roses. and then say to yourself, "boy I hope these weeds turn into roses one day". That makes absolutely no sense at all. You must completely understand that anything that's not like your purpose absolutely must go, although this is a hard principle you cannot afford the weeds. Yes, I am driving the point hard, when I say anything that's not like you, I mean just that - anything.

Please take this note. You must take measurement and an assessment of what energies are around you. Something can be good in your estimation, but if it's different, it is not good for you. A good thing can still be aligned with a weed.

Why?

Because it can still choke the life out of your personal intentions and your purpose. This applies especially to family members. This applies to boyfriends and girlfriends. This, moreover, and more importantly applies to husbands and wives. Anything that's not like where you want to go cannot grow in the same space of your destination.

Here's a fact That you must readily recognize. While you're sitting there hoping that somebody will change towards the direction of your intention because you love them, you must recognize like a weed that they are already grown. That means for the most part, people are locked into who they are. Those weeds still need to be pulled. This is something you don't want to play with or assume this to not be true. You do not want to wait five or ten years to know that what I'm telling you is a fact. Again, it's like looking at a bed of weeds and hoping one day those weeds will convert into roses. Worse yet, we give those weeds our undivided attention, so the weeds get the same nurturing and water as the roses. This makes absolutely no sense. Do not play with your life by expecting people to change to accommodate your vision. They have already grown into what they are.

It is only by these principles of growth that you will automatically grow extensively and bear fruit. Notice I used the word automatically. This is the way agriculture works. The farmer puts in the correct requirements and nurturing into the ground of whatever seeds he has planted. That's the work that needs to be done. When it comes to relationships and our personal growth, we put the work or the energy of work in the wrong place. When you take care of the ground, you do not have to take care of the growth. My God, we put the work into the relationship versus putting the work into the ground.

Here it is. If you're working on your relationship, you are doing the wrong thing. A relationship is about what's invested in you so you can grow. People must see that at the inception of your relationship. You never work to get to that point. That's a misplacement of the work that needs to be done. If your dreams are not naturally being nurtured by the people who say they love you, you need to be out of that relationship, because under those conditions you will not grow. This is a fact.

We work to get people to see our dreams. We work to get people to understand us. We work to get people to say good things about us. We work to get people to believe in us. We work to get people to stop for a minute to prioritize us. We work for attention. No!!! You work towards your vision and the people around must automatically nurture you. Pour into you. If they are not a farmer in your life, they are weeds growing up around you with their own intentions, ways, ideas, drama, conflict, and trauma. Their mere existence is choking out your greatest future!

Cut it out! Pull it up! Throw it in the garbage. When you are properly watered and nurtured, then your future doesn't need work. It will automatically produce the fruit of your purpose.

The Art of Becoming

Growth is about becoming. When you define your purpose or when you define your intention, you are defining what you're becoming. With that, you are also defining your future. This is the point where you have pierced the ground because the ground has been nurtured and watered. Just like a seed that has germinated becomes a tree that produces fruit, you are also in a state of becoming.

To remind yourself, always ask yourself the question what are you becoming?

Under the notion of becoming, there's still a point of horticulture that's needed at this point. It is called pruning. In the world of horticulture and agriculture as a tree or any type of plant is becoming what it is, in order to get it to produce more fruit you have to prune the growth that's not working for you. This is a very personal process, because it is not about anybody else, it's strictly about you.

What is it about you that will cause you to produce less fruit?

Let's look at some of the possibilities.

1. Belief in yourself.
2. Self-doubt.
3. Fear of the unknown.
4. Fear of being judged.
5. Fear of change.

These are five basic things that most people struggle with, but within their struggle they move to resolve or "fix" these issues. You must understand that this is the wrong application for these five items. The correct application for these five items is that they must be pruned. You do not resolve them, you do not fix them, you do not work your way past them. You don't need a psychologist, you don't need a psychiatrist, nor do you need any type of medication. These five items are a matter of pruning not a matter of resolving or fixing.

Be Rich in Knowledge

Here's the problem with believing in yourself. The concept of believing in yourself is an erroneous concept. There's no such thing psychologically as believing in yourself. Our biophysical systems contribute naturally to the direction that you choose to go. This is why I explicitly say that the first thing you do with anything, is that you have to design and define your future based on your desire. Then your biophysical system, which is your body, will automatically begin to convert what you just said in the context of your idea into a physical reality that is now memorized in your cells. Once something is memorized in your cells, you must know that that memory is a biophysical construct and not a mental construct. Now I know that's a lot, but it's a fact.

Belief is an attempt. That's why it's an erroneous concept. It's like being in the supermarket, and then saying to yourself, "I have to believe that I'm in the supermarket". It makes no sense, because now you're working at building a concept of being somewhere where you already are. It's like being born a girl, and then spending time trying to believe that you are a girl. It's like planting an apple tree, watching that tree grow over time, then watch that tree produce the apples, then grabbing that apple and biting it. But then somehow you have to tell yourself that I must believe that I'm biting an apple with all the proof in the world that that apple exists.

When someone tells you to believe in yourself, it is an erroneous ideology because you exist. In addition, everything that you build from your imagination immediately becomes a reality inside your body, so that future you constructed by your imagination exist. To turn around and then say I must believe that it's there, wipes out the conscious reality of your purpose and intention. Stop it!

This is not something that you work on, this is something that you cut out. As I said earlier, you must deal with life from a point of knowledge and not a point of belief. You must know that what you said as your purpose and intention is what's going to happen. Life responds to knowledge. Life does not respond to belief. That's why people must know you, not necessarily believe in you. Knowing who you are invokes a responsibility. Because when people know about you and your desire, then there's a responsibility to respond to that. You must be rich in knowledge about your greatness.

Be Rich in Trust

The opposite of doubt is the concept of trusting. What is trust? And what do you trust? Are you supposed to trust people? Are you supposed to trust what you see outside of yourself? Trust is intimately tied to knowledge. The issue with trust is that trust can be misplaced are displaced. I can even say this, "If you are believing, then essentially, you're not trusting." True trust is deeper than the concept of believing. In reality, trust can only be associated with knowledge. But here's the gift, you decide what you want to know.

People can tell you that they believe in you, but then take no actions towards that "belief" or behave differently outside of that belief, which is a sign that they don't trust what's in you. Really, when people see your purpose and intention, because they have the capacity to see it, it is not necessary to tell you that they believe in you, because trust takes you beyond belief. Trust makes you take action. When you end up associating with a lot of people who don't take action towards your purpose and intention or your desire, that now becomes the reality in you, and that's what you experience as self-doubt.

You do not wake up one day with the feeling of self-doubt without an aggregation of actions that forces that doubt in you because the people around you don't trust. And you then live in this space of self-doubt, not because you doubt what's in you, it's because you don't have enough people around you that's taking action towards you. Again, this is not a space that you work out. This is not a space that you resolve. This is not a space that you negotiate. This is not a space where you hope that people will behave towards you differently someday. This is a pruning space. When people don't take the right actions towards you, you cut them out. To prune self-doubt, you prune the people. This is not a space where you work on yourself. This is not a space of personal development. This is not a space of spiritual development. You don't need prayer, candles, meditation, or counseling; you need the people out of your life that can't see and act towards your greatness. Jesus Christ was a systemic presence of action towards people, because of what He knew about their greatness. You must be rich in people that trust you. We all must be rich friends.

Be Rich in Knowing Your Future

Do you know why people are afraid of the unknown? Because there's no such thing. This is where you must get a deeper understanding of who you are as a seed in the Earth. Using the example of an apple tree, it's like taking a seed out of an apple, planting it in the ground, and then say, "I have no idea what this tree is going to be". It makes absolutely no sense at all. A seed is the basis of what's coming in the future or what's becoming. This is about knowledge.

Once you have designed and defined your desire, from a human standpoint, it is now a seed. The "happening" or the growth is naturally imminent. What you planted on the inside from a horticultural standpoint is now an immediate fact. When a woman experiences conception and her egg, which is the seed is fertilized, although a zygote, the reality of the baby is immediate. At this point, you are dealing with something that you know. Knowledge changes everything.

Life Follows After Knowledge

When you define and design your design, you are dealing with the known. What you think you don't know, is how to get there. Getting there is a natural occurring fact that you don't have to concern yourself with, because the mechanisms of converting the imagination into a fact that you can experience, are not only built into your body but it's built into the Earth. What I'm saying is this, both your body and the Earth will naturally respond to your greatness. What you might be experiencing, that you're now calling the unknown, is the crazy actions that people take around you that gives you that feeling that you don't know how to get to where you're going. The doubt launches from the diminished investments that come from others. Changing the quality of your relationships changes what you know.

The natural flow is this. First, you establish the vision, then when people respond to your vision, your vision becomes imminent. Be rich in knowledge.

Be Rich in Confidence

A lot of people spend a great deal of time being extremely concerned about what others think about them. Now this is valid. Some would say, learn to ignore what people have to say about you or what they think about you. This seems to be solid advice, but it is the wrong advice. What people think about you is actually very important. It is a natural part of how life works, but you must understand how to manage it. That's right, value the thoughts of others towards you, but in addition, you must manage it because it is a value driven phenomenon. You are designed to intake the personal opinions of others about you. And yes, you should care.

Here's how it works. Definition comes from you in terms of who you are, but value comes from others. This sounds entirely different from anything you've ever heard before. How people see you, and thus, how people act towards you or respond to you, is a vital life force that is necessary. Remember, it is equivalent to the water that plants receive. The nurturing and care that comes from others is what is at the core of your personal growth. You must manage what comes into you, moreover, you must manage what's invested into you. As I said earlier, this is a matter of pruning. When you're not getting the right nurturing or care, it is a responsibility to remove diminished attention. I would go as far to say, when you're holding on to the person that's giving you wrong attention or diminished attention, you are blocking the right person from coming in.

Just like a plant or a tree, or any other type of vegetation suffers when there's not enough water and nutrients coming in, your confidence will suffer when you don't receive the right attention. What do I mean by this? One of the greatest fears that a person might experience is the fear of being judged. Most would think that this is verbal judgment. Yes, this is a form of judgment, but any action taken towards you under the guise of attention is judgment. How people treat you reveals what people think about you.

This space of judgment, whether it's verbal are through the actions of others becomes your story. I used to visit my auntie when I lived in North Carolina, and she had two different fruit trees in her backyard. Me and my auntie's niece would climb the trees in her backyard. She had several beautiful fruit trees and among these trees were orange trees and grapefruit trees. We climbed the orange tree and began tasting the oranges, but the oranges tasted like grapefruit. You can imagine that because the orange trees tasted like grapefruit, the grapefruit tree was the dominant tree that would affect what took place in other trees. Here's my point, people's judgment of you becomes who you are. This is why judgment is so important, karma but in addition, you must manage that space.

Change Your Story

When you get to the place wherein the diminished thoughts and actions of others write your story, you change your story by changing your environment. This leaves me right back to moving from the environment of the critical thoughts of my mother to the environment of my grandmother who invested in me a different story. Don't fear the judgment of others that will cause you to lose your confidence. Move into the environment and spaces wherein people hold you at a high value. You do not need to take confidence courses, nor do you need to do confidence exercises, or get counseling to help in the space of your esteem. You simply surround yourself with people who can correctly see who you are. To change your story you must:

1. Hear different things.
2. See different things.
3. Taste different things.
4. Touch different things.
5. Feel different things.

More importantly,

6. You must say different things. This is now your new story.

You are committing yourself to a different environment. Be rich in confidence.

Be Rich in Change

Comfort zones are your greatest enemy. When it comes to the subject of growth, you are also dealing with the subject of change. The fear of change is the greatest of all fears that invoke the greatest disability. If you're not changing, you're not growing. Using the example of trees, plants, and other types of vegetation, they do not reach their destination of purpose without change. For example, let's take any type of fruit tree, in order to get to the point wherein that tree bears fruit, it goes through multiple stages of growth. I would like to call these stages conversions.

Every phase of a plant's growth is a conversion. Think of the time that you were in your mother's womb, there were many stages of gestation that took place. If you didn't go through the stages or points of conversion, you would never be born. You cannot reach the destination of your purpose without converting within different stages. Quite simply, when you're unwilling to change, you will stunt your growth. This is why I say that your comfort zones are your greatest enemy.

Your Comfort Zones
Are Your Greatest Enemy!

Once again, this takes us right back to relationships. We allow our environment of relationships to force us into a space of not changing when it's necessary.

How is this?

When the people around you are not growing, it becomes entirely impossible for you to grow. This relationship environment becomes your comfort zone. You must change your environment, to change your story. In the same way, you must change your relationship environment, so you can make the necessary changes to reach your intent of purpose. People who change and grow will provide you the constant and consistent groundwork for the changes you need to make to reach your desired destination.

Change is necessary. Be rich in change.

The Space of Your Greatness

The space of your greatness is equivalent to the space of your environment. You must take measurement of your environment, first in order to grow, and secondly for you to reach the destination of your purpose. This is a measurable space, and you must take measurement of what's taking place within this environment. I will share with you a few tips on measurement. What I'm saying in addition, is that you must be aware of your environmental construct.

1. Make sure you are supported.

Everyone needs support, but everyone doesn't realize at times when they're not supported. This must become a space of awareness. Sometimes we are so good at taking care of ourselves that we don't realize when we're not being taken care of. The do-it-yourself mentality is not a badge of honor. As a matter of fact, this ideology could be very damaging, because your body and its emotional system, which is an extreme part of your personal biology, is designed to be supported. Active support from others registers in your cells, which in turn causes your body to operate in optimum health. Self-care is not recognized by the same biological protocols within your body. You are designed to be cared for. Please understand the importance of this.

Self-care as an ideology seems to be noble, but it is an erroneous concept. Even the Bible says it is not good for man to be alone. Our relationships are vital not only to your personal health, but it is also vital to the health of your ability to accomplish what you want in life.

2. Make sure people allow space for your personal growth.

Be careful with the "always telling you what to do" type people. There are people who always have something to say about what you're doing and where you are going. If you pay close attention, a lot of people who have a lot to say don't have much going on with their own life. These types of people will choke out your future potential. You must be allowed the room to grow without somebody in your ear all the time saying do it like me.

The only people that are qualified to speak into your well-being, are the people who are already in the space of where you're trying to go. That's called a mentor. Even a mentor, although his words are more valuable, will always give you the space to grow.

3. Make sure you are reinforced through verbal praise.

You need to hear good things about yourself. Once again, this is the water that contributes to your growth. The language towards you is also an environment. You must manage this language. Stay away from critical people. Stay away from people who constantly and consistently have negative things to say. You need to create an environment wherein you are praised constantly. It's like a healthy diet, you need affirmation, you need compliments, you need verbal encouragement, and you need words that align with your vision.

4. Make sure that you are "afformed" based on your personal affirmations.

What people say towards you immediately becomes a biophysical fact in you. The reality that comes from the words and actions of others will definitely impact your ability to progress and grow. Affirmations are good, but those affirmations must be supported through the confirmations of others. This is how life works. So, add this word to your vocabulary, Afformation.

You must require that the closest people to you must have the highest standards towards you. This includes how they treat you, how they act towards you, what they think about you, and what they say about you. I'm talking about husbands, wives, boyfriends, girlfriends, and especially close family. These are the people that have an immediate impact on the state of who you are. How your core relationships play out, translates into how your community of relationships play out. It all starts at the core. What's bad and close to you, will become the template of your larger community.

We all must be rich friends so that can become the standard of how everything else work in your life.

4 *Finish Rich*

It's a process getting to a finish line or reaching a desired destination. When you have a dream, and then to maintain that dream in your mind only, it is wholly insufficient when it comes to the subject of accomplishment. Many people start projects and never finish them. Not finishing what you start is beyond procrastination. This is stopping a project and never restarting that project to reach a finish line.

Has that ever been the case for you?

You must finish what you start. Having something in mind, and worse yet, starting it, but then never finishing is extremely damaging. There's a value in starting a dream and then finishing that dream. To more correctly state this, the real value is found in where you finish and how you finish. I will give you 8 motivations or reasons as to why you should finish your vision.

1. There's a high cost to not finishing.
2. Your "Why" must be strong.
3. You must set an example for the people who depend on you.
4. If you stop, starting again is like starting over.
5. Make the journey vital.
6. The "Apple Inc" theory. There must be excellence all the way through.
7. Don't start without knowing your finish line is at the top.
8. Create a sense of exclusivity.

There's A High Cost to Not Finishing

Everything in life is financial in nature. In a major sense, there's a cost to everything you do and there's a price to pay. Your vision or desired destination has value. As stated before, you must be the first to value the things that come through your mind. You must value your idea. Secondly, the people that you choose to participate in life must value you by valuing what's in you.

There's a financial term called appreciation. The word appreciation actually works in two different ways or two different modes. You have appreciation wherein you are thankful, then you have appreciation wherein something goes up in value. In both cases, appreciation applies here. Moreover, they work directly in conjunction with each other. Allow me to explain what I mean.

When you invest in the stock market, your desire would be for your investment to appreciate in value. The same goes for when you buy a home, it should appreciate in value overtime. The same goes for the idea that you have in your head or an intention that you have in mind. In order for what you think to appreciate in value, a transaction has to be made. This transaction is taking the idea or intention and moving forward on that idea and intention by taking action. Your idea and intention must be transferred from within to without. As you move towards the finish line of completing that idea or intention, there's a cost that is assessed along the way. In addition, once you're finished, there's a value assessed to your finished product.

At an early age, I earned my associate degree in nursing. It was time to graduate to higher levels as far as nursing was concerned. I wanted to add more value to what I was doing, so in this case I had to further my education. I signed up for school and was going for my master's degree. In this particular case, the program for both degrees were self-paced. Most people that participated in this bachelors and master's program could earn their degree in 18 months or maybe a little longer. Well, since it was self-paced, to save money I had planned to move through the program at lightning speed. And when I say lightning speed, that's exactly what I meant. Four months later I had moved through the entire program.

It was intense, but I finished what I started, and I did it in record time. In this case for me, it was about bringing down the cost. Quite obviously, the cost will be less by doing it in four months versus 18 months or longer. But the value in comparison to the other nursing students within the program was the same. I had the same degree that they had that held the same value, but I was able to reduce the cost by getting it done sooner than later.

But think about this, what if I didn't finish. Not only would the cost been high for the work that was already put in, but I couldn't gain value by finishing. Mainly because, in the end there would be nothing to appreciate in value. Here's where the second notion of appreciation must come in. That is appreciating or valuing what you have chosen to do. This must be done in the face of others when they don't have the same appreciation for what you decided to do.

When you feel like quitting or when you feel like moving slow, count up the cost first and then reinvigorate yourself towards reaching your goal and finishing what you started. Once again, what you finish will then appreciate in value overtime.

You must be rich in personal value!

Your "Why" Must Be Strong.

Another point of consideration that will drive you towards finishing what you start is that your "why" must be strong. This becomes a matter of consistency. A lot of people will start a journey, but within that journey can be highly inconsistent in their behavior or the actions that they take to finish that journey. The root of this inconsistency is that the reason to complete what they've started is not strong enough.

As a young child, I did not receive enough attention from my parents. This became my "why" for doing things differently. I took my pain and gave it a purpose. I use my circumstances as a child to influence my vision as an adult. Once again, this influence came from my grandparents, especially my grandmother. By moving in with them and having them to raise me, I had the opportunity to experience something greater, and then my strongest desire from that point on was to live in the space of that greater experience.

Take Your Pain and Turn It into a Purpose

I did not want others to experience the pain that I experienced as I was raised by my parents. So, my reasons for doing things in a more excellent way wasn't just for myself, but I wanted to provide the basis to where I could afford to give the attention that was needed to others around me. That became my reason. That became my "why".

Before starting any project, sit down and take the time to ask the why or the reason behind what you're deciding to do. Write it down. If it is not strong enough, you're in a space wherein you will be naturally inconsistent towards what you're attempting to do. Another way of putting this is that you have to have a strong story behind where you're going.

What is your story?

What is the story that is playing in the background of your personal efforts?

Is that story compelling enough to drive you towards your results? The why and the reason must be strong. Within this, there are two points of motivation. Pain can be a motivator, and your future desire can be a motivator. Both can work, but establishing a future desire is a more natural way to be consistent along the journey.

What do I mean by this?

I explained a little bit in the earlier chapters as to how your body plays a role in the accomplishment of anything that you desire. I will share a simple outline that you should be acutely aware of, because this will benefit you by knowing this particular truth, but I don't want to become too technical.

First, when you think of an idea are you have an innate desire to accomplish something, that idea is registered in all of your glands or your endocrine system. Most people think that memory is stored in the brain, but in actuality memory is stored in your body. Your body is the first thing that communicates your dream as hormones are passed to and from the glands in your body. It is amazing that when you create a future, moreover, a compelling future, your body immediately goes to work to accomplish that future.

Now, when you think about a painful point in your life, that event or circumstances is also a memory that is stored within your body. This memory impacts your nervous system and can also be a driving force as to why and how you decide to do things. But your body is not designed to use pain as a motivator. Your body is designed to use vision as a motivator. Simply put, it is better to run towards something than to run from something.

It Is Better to Run Towards Something Than to Run from Something!

This is why you must sit down and evaluate the reason why you have set a particular goal or intention. Essentially, you are designed to win, and you must document that "winning" well before you start your journey. This will take on being the driving force towards where you're going. The powerful motivation of the future will set in a natural consistency of behavior towards that future. Allow your purpose to drive you versus your pain. Once again, pain will work, but purpose is naturally a stronger motivator.

You have a natural story that will always contribute to what you decide to do. The opportunity here is this, you can rewrite a past story through writing a future story. The memory mechanisms of your body cannot differentiate between the past and the future, so when you write a stronger future story, the past story will naturally become diminished. Once again, this is a huge opportunity.

Some people have a horrible past, where is the opportunity in that?

The stronger the influence of the past, the stronger the story has to be written for the future. This simply means you have to outpace the memory of the past by creating a greater story for your future, this within itself gives you the basis for an outstanding future. Your past becomes an excuse to create a compelling future. I excelled at everything that I did because I remembered what my parents didn't do. It forced me to do things at a greater level.

You must do things at the highest levels. Your past can't become the reason to not do your best, it must be the reason that you will do your best. You can rewrite a future story that outweighs your past. The greater the past trauma, the greater your future reality. There's the opportunity.

Your story must be rich!

You Must Set an Example for The People Who Depend on You

In my family I am definitely the matriarch of the family. Naturally within the context of families, you have that go to person that everyone depends on. Well, that's me. Some people might take this on as a weight, but I take it on as a privilege. Going back to the story of how I was raised by my mom and dad, getting pregnant at an early age, and then not receiving the support that I needed from them, this became a pain that I didn't want any of my family to experience.

This became one of the reasons why I worked so hard at advancing myself, because the value that I set for myself was tied into how I valued the people in my family. For me, everything had to be done with extreme excellence. This not only gave me the means to provide for my family, but it also set an example to my family as to how things should be done. Like my grandmother, somebody has to take on the responsibility of being an example to influence the way how things should be done. I needed my family to see that.

I was completely driven to be successful, and this is why I became a stylist at an early age and became a nurse at an early age. First, I was not going to go back and be that person that everybody thought I would be as a young teenage mother. This was a motivating factor, but from this motivating factor I created a different motivating factor by deciding what I wanted to be. Not only was this personally important for me, that's one thing. But I had other people that depended on what I did or what I didn't do. In this, I gave my family a living story.

Why is this important?

You have heard the old adage, talk is cheap. You must realize how cheap "talk" really is. Words have minimal value, but pictures have extreme value.

Can you imagine me trying to convince my family to excel without having excelled myself?

Can you imagine the struggle trying to explain to everybody that you must be great at what you do without having done something great?

Can you imagine trying to convince other young ladies that your circumstances have nothing to do with what you can accomplish without accomplishing something?

I'm sure you get the point. Influence is done through example, not through words.

What you do is more readily transferred to others than what you say. This became my strongest reason for designing out a future for myself, which then became my point of focus. I was no longer running from the pain, but creating a future so my family can be influenced to do great things. In essence, your story will become the story of others around you. But you cannot tell the story, you must live the story.

Use your words to influence yourself, use the accomplishment of those words to influence the people you care about. Have a rich story to tell.

If You Stop, Starting Again Is Like Starting Over

Some people use a stop and go strategy to reach their end goal. If this is you, you will quickly find out that you'll never reach your end goal. Movement towards something that you have designed in your mind is essentially an energy. When you stop your movement.

That stopping is also an energy. Why am I describing these two notions as energy?

Energy is essentially based on motion. From a scientific point of view, work or motion at work is a great description for energy. Newton's first Law of Motion can be applied here. There is a cause to motion, and for things to be at rest, there is a cause there too. These are perpetual states whether you're moving or whether you're sitting still. Sitting still cannot be an option when you have a dream or a strong desire.

For you to understand this I have to give you the definition of perpetual. Perpetual in simple terms is something that repeats are reoccurs without effort. Now this is easily understood when it comes to things being in motion. It is easy to understand perpetual motion.

But what happens when you stop moving towards your goal?

The stopping becomes perpetual. That's why I call stopping energy. When you begin a journey towards a desired goal or intention and then you stop, you cannot even begin to imagine the damage that's being done when motion it's being brought to a halt. That "stopping" is an energy because the "stopping" is essentially in motion also.

What???!!!?

Here I must go back to how memory works along with your body. Remember when you design a compelling future your body remembers that future. The memory of your future is literally stored in cells within your body. I'm sharing this with you, because it's important for you to know some of this scientific information or biophysical information.

When you start a project, and at some point, stop a project or even slow down, this stopping is also memorized within your body as a biophysical fact. The cells within your body are in continuous motion, so when you decide to stop, the memory that your cells hold at that point will perpetuate the stopping. When somebody takes a narcotic or any type of addictive drug, that drug becomes a memory in the body. That's the basis of addiction. All memory is the basis of addiction. Your body and your nervous system will only do what it remembers to do.

The reason why it becomes difficult for people to overcome addictions, it is because that addiction is stored in the body and the drug or the narcotic is telling the body what to do. I am glad you understand that. When you commit yourself to completing a project, and then stop that project, you are now memorizing the "stopping". Then when you make the effort to try to start again, the "stopping" message will play against your effort to restart. Your nervous system is now working against you and not for you. The danger of stopping is the addiction of stopping.

Is this you?

Think about all the things that are just sitting around not done.

Why?

Stopping things becomes an addiction, therefore you're stopping is in perpetual motion. Think of the excuse as one might make to stop even for just a little while, not realizing the damage that stopping actually does.

There's a biblical story of a man named Gideon who was establishing an army, and as they journey towards the battlefield, everyone that stopped at different points was fired.

Why?

Because they would have brought the energy of stopping to the battle. Stopping creates the energy of stopping. Going back to the point of counting up the cost within the context of a journey, when you stop or even slow down, the cost is extreme.

This is why when you stop along the way, it will seem like when you want to start, it's like starting over again. Build a compelling story for your future and don't stop! You must be rich in your movement.

Make The Journey Vital

We talked about making the destination a valued fact that will appreciate overtime. But in addition, you must also value the journey. When working on my master's degree, I immediately assessed the cost over time to gain that degree. This motivated me to move through this particular journey at a much faster pace. When I was done, the university had to do rebates, because they did not expect me to finish so fast.

Here's the point, because I had assessed a value to my journey, others had to do the same. In addition to being completely surprised at the speed in which I accomplished my master's degree, they had to acknowledge that this had never been done before. It felt extremely wonderful to know that I had accomplished something that thousands of others had not accomplished. This is because I value the journey and within that value, I put in the hard work that was necessary to make getting my master's degree very special.

Value Your Journey

Another reason to value the journey in addition to reaching a particular goal, the structures of that journey can be applied to your new destinations. As a matter of fact, this application is a natural phenomenon.

What do I mean by this?

Your body does not just remember your future destination, once you accomplish that destination, it remembers the destination along with remembering how you got there. What you decide to do and finish becomes a fact inside your body. I can't overstate this enough, your nervous system and the cells within your nervous systems works on memory. If you had a great journey towards a particular destination, the journey becomes an addiction. Of course, we are talking about a positive addiction. Your body is naturally designed to be addicted, and when you do certain things that now become a memory within your body, your body or your nervous system will want to repeat those actions.

When you value the journey, that value will extend to all of your new journeys, and the new destination will become more naturally automatic. Meaning, it becomes easier to accomplish the next thing. Simply put, you not only become used to winning and accomplishing, but you will also become addicted to winning and accomplishing.

Here's where the second notion of appreciation comes in once again. You must appreciate the journey as well as the destination. This means you take notice of the things you do while you're doing them. It's learning from your mistakes and using your mistakes as opportunities to do things right the next time, and then value that right action. In this, you must not be afraid of taking action and moving towards your desired destination. You must not take into consideration your roadblocks, but only consider where you're going. Where you're going will teach you how to move past your roadblocks.

This is where writing, documenting, or journaling becomes vitally important. As you move along your journey, document key factors of your journey.

Why is this important?

When you write things down, the memory of that thing becomes more readily enforced as a memory. You need to use this memory to make all of your next actions. This is why you value the journey.

The third reason to value your journey is that it makes your accomplishments become more automatic. In reality, it's not so much about reaching goals than it is about taking action towards your goals. Actions will always produce some type of result. A great orientation of the journey will always produce great results. If you journal the journey, the great things that come out of the journey can be more readily applied to all of your future journeys.

A Great Direction Clarified Will Always Produce Great Results

Make your journey special. Enjoy the journey. Yeah, people will tell you that the journey should be rough, and there is struggle within the journey, and it's never easy to get to the top. But I want to refute those notions. If you pay attention to those who describe the journey this way, you will readily see that their results reflect the roughness. Their results reflect the struggle. Their results reflect things not being easy. So don't listen to those people. Make your journey special and assess value to that journey.

There are no brownie points given for things being hard. Once you set your mind to something, you don't have to build a "pre story" that things will be rough. Guess what, when you make that the reality, that's exactly what's going to happen. Why build a bad story before you start? It makes absolutely no sense at all. When you start something, do not start with the intention that things are going to be hard, things are going to be rough, things are not easy. That is a design. If that's your design, that's how things are going to be.

Yes, things are going to happen along the way that you do not desire, but if you set the intention to enjoy the journey and to assess value to that journey, you will move past those supposed problems much quicker than people who are anticipating problems. You must anticipate being past the problem. Anticipating problems will draw your focus towards just that - problems. You are then drafting a journey with problems.

You're not only pre planning your destination, but you are also pre planning your journey. Get excited about what's going to happen by designing what's going to happen. Your journey must be rich.

The "Apple Inc" Theory

In what you do, there must be excellence all the way through. When it comes to finishing what you start, focus on excellence. One of the most impressive companies that practices this theory is Apple Inc. I had recently bought an apple pencil and realized that the box that the apple pencil came in was extremely elegant. I could only imagine that apple probably spent as much money on the box and the packaging as it did on the pencil itself.

You can tell that this box was crafted and not just simply thrown together. The way the pen sat within the box was extraordinary. How you had to open the box by pulling out a box tucked in another box. This would naturally keep you from tearing the box open by creating a sliding mechanism to open the box. This is ingenious. It forces you to take an action that causes you to value the box as well as valuing what was in the box.

What does this do?

It causes you to value the company that made the box and the pen. Guess what?

Now you are poised to buy everything that Apple Inc has to sell. Another company that does this is Nike. Not only are their products made with excellence, but their packaging is also made with excellence. Here's why I'm describing the body and its memory systems in the context of this book. You are made with excellence. There's a biblical scripture that states that you are fearfully and wonderfully made. This means that everything that comes from you must be done with excellence. You are the original packaging to your future.

When you are putting together your product or service, you must plan for excellence all the way through. This excellence is immediately reflected back on you and your existence in the world. People must experience the value in what you create, which then causes them to see the value in who you are. This should be a natural notion, but people are drawn away from their own value based on how people treat them. It took my grandmother to establish value in me when my parents could not. Now the work that I do must display an excellence that I intend to transfer to others.

The title of this book, We Should All Be Rich Friends, is about establishing a network of values wherein excellence is exuded. I have established an organization or a community which is called, "Rich Friends Circle". This is the place where first, value is assessed within the context of a person's own greatness, then along with that assessed value, there's a community of rich friends that can help you maintain that value through networking. Your connections determine the space of your excellence.

Your Connections Determine the Space of Your Excellence.

This is why you find rich people hanging around rich people. On the opposite end, this is the same reason why you find poor people around poor people. Your connections create a perpetual existence. Your connections create what you repeat in life. If you want to repeat greatness, then you have to have a community of connections that express greatness in continuity and in perpetuity. We should all be rich friends. You cannot afford your starting points in life to be anything less than how you value yourself. It must show up in everything that you do starting with your connections.

This is what I call the Apple Inc Theory. The value of who you are will extend into the value of not only what you do, but it will extend into the value of what you produce. Every part of that production must show equal value. This is an extreme secret to life, and it's only a secret because people don't pay attention to it. What do the things look like that come from you? Moreover, not only must the things you create have an heir of excellence, but it must be capable of having an impact on other people.

People literally save their Apple computer boxes, their iPhone boxes, and their iPad boxes, because those boxes tell a story about the company. When it comes to the strategy of building your dream, which essentially comes from establishing a product that other people will buy, excellence must be seen and experienced all the way through and at every stage. Apple was smart enough to make opening up a box a grand experience. This creates a natural affinity to your creation.

Your ideas and the subsequent creation of those ideas must be a grand experience. With this, you are not chasing a clientele, but a clientele swears by your ability to create excellence. Your customer base becomes a natural phenomenon that extends from your space of greatness. You must be seen as rich!

Don't Start Without Knowing Your Finish Line Is at The Top

Where do you set your intentions when it comes to what you desire?

Allow me to answer that for you. For whatever genre of creation, you're in, to imagine being in anything less than the best that's in the world is a detriment to the accomplishment of that thing. In essence, never plan to be second place.

When it comes to your vision and your dream, you must have an Olympian attitude. Not one person that participates in the Olympics goes in with the plan of just winning second place. That notion will damage not only their ability to make the Olympics, but it also damages the journey.

Why would you establish a future, and then in any way limit that future?

When you don't place in mind a compelling end game, the journey that you take towards where you're going will automatically be affected.

Remember when it comes to consistency, there must be a compelling reason to be consistent. Otherwise, there will be a tendency to slack off simply because of not placing the highest value or importance on the destination. You must remember that your destinations are a reflection of who you are. Your creations are a reflection of who you are. Destinations and creations launch off of the space of what you think, more importantly, how you think. Remember, the boxing and the packaging, which is a reflection of your journey, has to be done well and with the intention of winning at the top of your game.

When it comes to being in business, especially if you are a new business, people have to have a reason to switch from what they're doing to what you have to offer. You are responsible for giving them that reason. If you are #2, that within itself is a reason to not use your products or services. Plus, you are telling on yourself. If you don't value yourself and the things that come from you, it simply means you also don't have the capacity to value who you're serving. Apple became the biggest company in the world, because when people bought their stuff, they felt valued.

When you set this energy as a standard, this alone will drive you to finish what you start. Because you will be so excited about what you are creating, you can't wait to get it done. In addition of not being able to wait to get it done, you can't wait for people to experience your creation. You must be rich in how you serve. Moreover, people must "feel" rich when they engage in your creation.

Create A Sense of Exclusivity

My rich friend's community is an extremely special space. In the space of this community, I deployed the secrets that maintain an internal value that causes everyone within that community to be rich. Let's make this very simple. There's a reason why some people are rich and others are not. Generally, when you meet a person that is not only rich, but extremely wealthy, there is definitely a community behind that wealth. Here's the secret. The reason why people don't know about these communities is because these communities are essentially exclusive, and there's a reason behind the exclusivity.

You might ask, what is that reason?

The reason is, not everyone is prepared for excellence. You cannot mix excellence with mediocrity.

In my space, I have a circle of rich friends, but not everybody is able to join this circle, because you must have the mindset of wealth that is built on excellence. We should all be rich friends, because we should all be thinking from the same space of creativity. And you definitely need a community that matches this particular system of values.

This is what I use in my circle. There is a process in joining. There is a cost in joining. An assessment is made with every applicant. The reason is, is that in this rich friend circle, there's not space and time to make you feel valuable, you must know your value coming in, because your value will add to the value of others, wherein from the connection of those values things will grow exponentially.

In everything that you do, it is naturally done in the space of who you connect with and how you connect. If you value your future and you want to reach the goals of your intention, you must make the space around you and exclusive space. Not everybody can get in. This within itself is a value, because you know how to keep things out that can't contribute value.

Exclusivity is not selfishness; exclusivity is a way of distancing yourself from distraction. Think of your relationships that are directed towards what you want to accomplish as a club, and everyone in this club must be ultra focused on where you're going. Your club is a system of like minds with like levels of accomplishment. If you want your creations to be ultimately special, then the people around you have to be special, and you must hold that as a requirement. This enforces a value amongst the whole.

This is something that you have to be smart enough to be the case well before you involve yourself with anybody. This is the gift of assessment. Assessment that causes exclusivity. Don't let people make you feel guilty when you decide that they can't be involved with what you're doing and where you're going. There's the old adage, not everybody can go with you. This is absolutely true, but you don't want to find out that people can't go with you through the experience of connecting with them, then something goes bad, and then you have to get rid of them. Make what you do and your creations and exclusive notion now and not later.

Exclusivity enables you to finish what you start, because you are not distracted by "people energy" that's not like where you are going. Be Rich in Likeness and Likeminded.

5 Be Rich In Imagination

I was talking to my son. He just got back from Colombia, and he was talking about how tired he was. You know coming back from customs and all that was pretty difficult. He said, "when I vacation, I really like to just chill, but my wife, she wants to go and do things, and it's like she wants to get everything out because when she goes back home you know it's back to the grind."

I told my son; I imagine a life where I don't have to take a vacation. When I go out of the country, for me it's not a big thing. I don't really do it for the experience, but well, I do it for the experience, but not to vacation, because I don't vacation for my life. I'm ready to get back home. I've been there done that kind of thing. If I'm there for a day, I'm good. I don't have to see everything, because I imagine my life the way it is now at home. I'm just living it in 3D, but it's all simply imagination.

I really created a life where I don't have to vacation. People think this is a resort where I live. Where I live is a product of my imagination. I have my tennis courts and all the amenities right here in my neighborhood, and I don't have to go to take a vacation. I told him that the 911 that I drive right now came from my imagination first. When I got the car, it wasn't like I had this feeling that I got it, because I was already driving the car before in my imagination. That's what imagination in my life.

One of the biggest creations I've been imaging is my rich friend's community of 3000 plus. The value of a community is beyond extraordinary. There are masterclasses inside my community that drive individuals directly towards their desired goals. In addition, because it is a community, there's a wealth of resources among the members itself. The power of community is extraordinary because you do not have to put in the work to find people on your level of imagination. The vetting and assessments of individual intentions have already taken place due to the exclusiveness of the organization.

For the optimization of your imagination, you must avail your level of thinking to a space where your imagination and brilliance can garner consistent agreement and support. My circle of rich friends is a superior starting point.

Imagination is a gift. It is what sets you apart from the rest of Earth's species. When you think, you think in pictures. These pictures could come from the following two sources.

1. The environment.
2. Your imagination.

Let's look a little closer as to how the environment can structure your imagination. For billions of years biology has been controlled, pushed, and influenced by the environment. A better way to explain it is where outside circumstances or situations influence behavior and determination. The first single cell's movement was influenced by light. Climate has an impact, whether things are hot or whether things are cold, dark or light, all of life responds to outer environments. Here are some additional environmental concerns that have an influence on your thinking and behavior.

1. Learning or anything that causes you to learn.
2. What others have to say.
3. Others' opinion of you. Thoughts towards you. How someone feels about you.
4. Someone's behavior towards you. Your relationships.
5. Time.
6. Events.
7. Sound, heat or cold, or anything that impacts the 5 senses.

All of these items can be considered external governments. Again, they are anything that's outside of you that impacts your thinking and impacts your movements or behavior. Not only does most of the animal kingdom operate off external principles, better yet, a majority of their learning comes from outside influences. As humans, a majority of our learning comes from the seven sources that I listed above.

You and I can go one step beyond these seven major influences or environmental concerns. That one step beyond is your imagination. This is where we can draft pictures based on a future desire. As I mentioned before, this is an extreme gift, and it is a unique gift.

Let's call the seven items above circumstances. In general, circumstances control a person's thinking and behavior. But that's not the end. A person or a human being has the capacity to think beyond their circumstances. Not only is this a gift but it is an opportunity. You're not limited to the things that happen to you because you can always choose beyond those things by creating something new. Let me break it down this way.

I – Mage

Or

I – Dea

An image or an idea is something that you can create beyond your five senses, and more importantly beyond any circumstance that might happen. Circumstances constitute an environment because of the nature of its influence. You can bypass any influence by reimagining something greater than the circumstance.

Respect for Your Imagination

The root word of image is -mage. This is where we get the English word magic. It is also where we get the English word magistrate. Both the definition of magic and magistrate perfectly illustrate how powerful the word image is. Moreover, they demonstrate how powerful the word imagination is.

Magic is when one can take something that is generally not seen or understood, bring it from the place of being unseen to being seen. This is the perfect purpose of imagination. What happens in the mind is typically unseen, but if you can produce what's in the mind outside of your mind, it becomes a seen phenomenon. This is magic.

Magistrate has more to do with power. Depending on the culture, magistrate can be a judge or a king. Both denote power. Generally, a judge's ruling is final, and people will have to abide by or obey a judge's ruling. As a matter of fact, a king in medieval times held that same power, because the king also served as a judge when it came to disputes.

Both of these apply directly to your imagination or your ability to imagine. It is a responsibility to take what you see for your future and produce that future into a seen phenomenon. At the same time, you must respect your imagination from the standpoint of a judge. What you see is final. Once you establish a future imagination for yourself, you must protect that imagination from all other influences. This is the only way that you can make the magic happen.

Another power that the king had in medieval times is his court. This simply means that whatever came to the King's mind, at a snap of a finger, it was served. It could have been food, it could have been a command to go build something, it could be a command to bring somebody to his presence, or it could be a simple command for entertainment. Whatever the king thought that was subsequently said, people jumped on it. The same must go for your imagination. When you speak out your dreams and intentions for your future, the people around you must have enough respect for you to respond to your desires immediately.

The third value that a magistrate brings to the table is the value of expansion. Most kingdoms had provinces or territories. These provinces and territories abided by whatever happened at the castle. Whatever the laws were set in the castle was also abided by in the territories and provinces. A King's job was to expand his territory by having his army go out and take over lands.

When you have an imagination, or as I stated earlier, you have a compelling future designed for yourself, you need for others to take on that same design, which then will become a natural expansion of yourself. They become your province. You need for others to become an extension of what you know about yourself, moreover, what you imagine about yourself and your future. A lot of people try to do things independently, but that's not how true imagination works. Imagination needs a team to respond to that imagination and then become part of that imagination, so the reality of your intention becomes imminent because you lock into outside provinces or territories. The true way of expansion is through your connections that are like you.

Magic happens through your connections. This is how a king or queen gets things done. They can say the word and be rest assured that something 100 miles away will be done exactly to their specifications. With this being the case, you need people who hold the capacity to respond correctly to what you imagine for your future. Here are some of the responses that you don't need. It's important to know these because you would need to take measurement of how people respond to your imagination. If they don't agree, that's not OK. In medieval days that was handled by chopping off heads. You might not want to go that far, but you do need to at least chop the relationship off.

1. Why don't you try something easier?
2. Child that's too much.
3. Here's what I think.
4. Why don't you try this first? Or why don't you try that first?
5. How are you gonna make that happen?
6. I don't think you can do that.
7. What will people think?

When it comes to your imagination, you will quickly find that the people who have the least will naturally have the most to say. Usually what is said will stand against your intentions and you cannot afford that. Some of these responses might be extremely subtle, but pay attention to how people respond to what you dream about. Anything that's not like your dream is extremely destructive, because nothing gets done when there's two or more different directions.

You must be the first to value your imagination. If you don't respond to your dreams at the highest level, how do you expect others to respond correctly?

Here's a few things that you can do to lock in your imagination or your dream.

1. As soon as you get a picture in your head as it concerns your future, write it down.
2. Next, begin to associate the right people that you might know that has a potential connection to what you've written down. This will almost immediately exclude most family members. Don't be afraid of this. You need people that are like what you see. Moreover, you need people who can hear what you see.
3. Connect with those people and build those relationships exclusively.
4. Create strong conversations around your imagination.
5. In whatever way you can, begin to take action towards your imagination.

Your relationships and actions that you take determine the level of respect that you garner around what you see for your own future. Again, do not be the first to diminish or discount the value of what you see for yourself. You will have plenty of people to do this for you without you doing it.

Again, the idea is to move what's in your head out of your head for experience. Not only for the experience of yourself, but for others to experience also. As you practice these things, you will become the consummate professional at making magic happen. Magic is essentially an energy, and when you can build this type of energy of accomplishment around you, it will draw more people to you and towards what you have to offer. Just like a king is known in all the land, you'll become known for the person that can make magic happen.

Respect for Your Idea

The root word of idea is -dea, which means "to see". As I mentioned earlier, we see in pictures. Of course. But in addition, we think in pictures. I want you to think of thinking as a way of seeing or thinking as seeing. Just like with the imagination, you must respect what you see. This is also a gift, because you can always see beyond your circumstances. Although I'm sharing the gift of seeing or the gift of your ideas second, your ideas are closely related to imagination. Imagination is about getting what you see outside of yourself. But seeing is the most important part of this formula.

From the very beginning of this book, we talked about your desires. It is important to have a desire, because to desire something is a vital life force. A desire speaks from the expanse of your feelings, and how you feel is simply a chemical composition in your body. Here again we must bring back those items that operate from outside of you in which we would call your external government or your external environment. Your external environment will speak to your body, your body will form a chemical composition that gives you a feeling in response to the environment. This in turn, will control the pictures that take place in the space of your mind. This is why feelings proceed thoughts.

The strategy here is to come up with ideas outside of environmental concerns. If your idea is stronger than the environment, your body will build the chemicals or feelings to your ideas versus the environment. It's almost like reversing the process, but you're not waiting for external concerns to influence what you think hard to put ideas in your head, you start with the ideas which will in turn cause your body to respond. What you need to know at this point, your body will begin to control your environment. This is the power of an idea. This is why you must respect your ideas because your ideas reversed the order of nature. Nature does not rule you, but your ideas rule nature.

Nature does not rule you, but your ideas rule nature.

Like imagination, your ideas must be immediately supported by the people that are around you. Your ideas must be immediately supported by the people who consider themselves to care about you. With ideas being so powerful, you cannot risk having an aggregation of people around you that is different from your idea. The external government of people is a powerful force, and for the most part will be the first energy that will convince you to discount your idea.

-dea means to see. Deity means light or to shine. Which means to see the light is to see the mind of God. The 14th century meaning of idea was to see the mind of God. So, here's the match.

Your Idea Is a Point of Light.
Your Idea Is I – Deity.
What's Released from You
Is the Way People See God!

When you think about the word idea, you must think of it from the standpoint of what you see in yourself that not only lights your path but becomes a light for others to see. Again, respect the idea that comes to mind, because what comes to mind will then be recorded in your body. Your body now holds the intelligence to control the environment. From a biophysical standpoint, the environment is designed to follow your thinking. You are not designed to follow the environment.

One of the greatest things that I've learned is that when you don't create a future for yourself, moreover, if you don't think for yourself, then others will think for you. Or your circumstances will think for you. Your environment will think for you. You will live under the power of other people's ideas and imagination. Here's what's horrible about this, when you live under the power of other people's ideas or imagination, usually you're paying for it.

In general, society or the powers to be did not want you to think for yourself, because it becomes a huge financial windfall to sell you something to assist you in your thinking. Let's go back to my son and his vacation. Because of the power of my imagination, my vacations follow me. Someone put a nice ad on TV about a very nice vacation spot, and guess what? You had to shell out some money to get there. They sold you an image and then you had to pay for it. This is the cornerstone of commercialism, convincing you by telling you what you should see.

Once you have settled in an idea, you can use your imagination to begin to experience that idea. This is an acute energy that works on your behalf. Here are a few things that you can do to lock down your ideas.

1. Like the imagination, write down your ideas immediately.
2. Begin to build energy around your idea by sharing your idea only with those who have the capacity to act upon your idea. This is a simple concept, if you came up with an idea for a pastry, it will fall on deaf cars if you're talking to a medical doctor about it. Create the energy by talking to the right person. Begin the conversations.
3. Now take notes on the conversations. These notes will begin to give you direction as you dialogue within the space of your idea. This dialogue will begin to create the expansion or the energy for expansion. Once again, talking to the wrong people will kill your idea immediately. Do not start at dead ends.
4. To keep your initial ideas hot, always expand on your idea, because all ideas are meant to grow. So, never limit yourself to the possibilities of your idea.
5. Create a lifestyle or a desired lifestyle. What I mean by this is write down what type of car you want to drive, what type of house do you want to live in, how do you want to travel, where

do you want to travel. Decide how much money is coming in on a monthly basis.

What this does is give your ideas a place to go. Because you have a desire for a lifestyle, that idea can get you to that lifestyle, because you begin to associate a financial value to your idea. Here is how and where your ideas become real. The bigger the lifestyle you want, the larger your idea has to be. It is a lifestyle that will give you the feelings, and the feelings will drive your ideas. This is why it's important to create a lifestyle that will be a result of your idea.

You Must Assess a Financial Value to Your Idea!

Whenever you experience something that you're not satisfied with, allow your imagination and your ability to create an idea to outpace that dissatisfaction. This is something that can happen immediately. This is also something that you can become an expert at doing. For the most part, when your imagination and idea is so compelling, anything that happens within your environment becomes inconsequential. You are so locked into your imagination that what others have to say doesn't matter. What other people do to you doesn't matter. What the weather outside is doesn't matter. Your circumstances doesn't matter, because you use your imagination and power to create ideas to influence the circumstances, versus the circumstances influencing you.

Creating the Environment for Your Imagination and Ideas

Another word used for this space, the space of your imagination and ideas, is creativity. Here's where a lot of people have problems. They will immediately say that they are not creative in nature. This is a dangerous mindset. What they are actually saying is that they can't think for themselves, and truly, there is a population of people that will never be able to think for themselves. These are the people that need jobs, simply because they need instruction. And that's OK.

These are also the same people that respond to every element or wind that blows. Their mechanism of creativity is dead in the face of their circumstances. Creativity or creation is a natural part of the human experience. Yes, I said it. If you are not in the space of creating, you're missing the greatest part of the human experience. Not only does this get you the things that you desire, but it also enables you to bypass problems that other people can't bypass. You can always create beyond chaos.

Creating beyond chaos is a natural phenomenon. Just as with imagination and ideas, creation is a huge opportunity. As a matter of fact, your creative ability causes chaos to be a benefit. In a lot of cases come with the level of chaos causes a forced level of creativity. The bigger the problem that has to be solved, the bigger the idea or the greater the imagination has to be. Chaos pushes you higher when you access your creative ability. But most people don't do this. At the onset of chaos, they create a relationship with the chaos, and then ignore their potential to immediately build a presence beyond the chaos. With this, when you acknowledge your creativity, or when you acknowledge your ability to come up with an idea, or acknowledge the space of your imagination, chaos becomes a friend.

Your Creative Ability
Causes Chaos to Be a Benefit.

As a matter of fact, when you design an intention for your future, that intention becomes a prepared consciousness that will drive you past circumstances well before those circumstances meet you. This is why it is vital to come up with designs for your life, because those same designs would naturally outpace even the things that have not happened yet. Your future design prepares you to meet obstacles head on, because you know that what you see for your future is more important than what's in front of you.

These type of people are typically not moved by external circumstances or external governmental concerns. They have already won way before the trouble gets there. Their creativity already outweighs any future concerns.

Here are a few ways to create an environment for natural innovation or creation.

1. Hang around people who are always creating something and innovating.

2. Always have an intention for something new. Never wait on something new or next, be the one who is the creator of what's new and next.

3. As in the last chapter, when you have an idea, complete that idea. Complete what you see. Upon completion, new ideas and points of creativity will automatically pop up. Finishing something will generate more ideas.

4. Have a pencil and a piece of paper or some type of recording device next to you when you go to bed. For the most part, ideas pop up at this time and you must be ready to lock them down immediately. The worst thing to happen is for your mind to generate this wonderful idea, and then you say, well I'm going to write it down in a few, and by the time you get ready to write it down, the idea is gone.

5. Always generate the energy to start an idea. Immediately do something towards your idea. This will generate the energy, wherein your idea will start speaking back to you.

6. Never get help on coming up with an idea, only get help to facilitate an idea. Getting help to come up with an idea exposes you to other energies that will automatically have something to say whether it's a value or not.

7. Learn to sit still and let ideas come to you. There is something in you that is already generating greatness. Always be prepared to hear your own greatness.

8. Surround yourself with idea generators by seeking a community of idea generators.

I = Magic
You are Magic.
You are Your Imagination
I = Dea
I = What You See
What You See is Who You Are

The value of your ideas and your imagination is equivalent to your personal value. This is why I will always say, never discount what comes to your mind. Because you are essentially discounting who you are. When you value your greatness, it becomes easier for others to value who you are. Your greatness starts by designing your future desire.

Be rich in imagination.

Be rich in ideas.

6 Be Rich in Results

Now that you know the importance and the power of your imagination and ideas, you must take action on what you see. Both notions of imagination and ideas are a matter of what you see and how you see. You think in pictures, thus you create what you see by taking acute action towards what you see.

You'll be surprised at the amount of actions that you might take during the course of the day that has nothing to do with what you have set as an intention as far as your imagination is concerned. Under this paradigm of behavior, you cannot achieve the results you are expecting. Results are vital to your personal existence. At the risk of sounding extremely simple, I will state this as a fact; all of life is about results.

All of Life Is About Results.

Think about it. Everything that you see is a result of some type of action that has been taken. Moreover, when it comes to the subject of creation, every result has its start as a picture in someone's bank of memory. Someone had to picture the creation before the creation existed for experience. There is a creator, which is you. Then you have creatures, which is the rest of biological phenomena. Creatures do not create, which means their behavior patterns, once born, are set for life.

As a creator, you can desire then define and design a creation. This space of definition and designation is unlimited in scope and possibility. This gift of being without limits comes with a responsibility. That responsibility is the necessary actions that align with your creations. The space of creation happens first as a picture, then as the actions towards that picture to achieve the result of the picture.

Why is this important?

You must monitor and measure your actions. Why? A lot of actions that a person might take are creature based and not creator based.

What do I mean by this?

Actions taken from the pictures that you develop from your imagination or the ideas you create, move into the space of being created. Actions taken as a result of your circumstances and outside influences make you a creature, not a creator. You must choose a life or a lifestyle; are you a creature or are you a creator? You are designed naturally to be results oriented, but if you're driven by everyday external governments and circumstances, you are regulated to being just a creature. This exposes you to a series of poverty level experiences and primitive cycles of life.

Practice dreaming and creating. Practice getting results. Your results not only serve you personally, but your results are meant to serve others. From the corporate perspective, you have the giants of the industry such as Apple Inc, Microsoft, Walmart, Amazon, Space X, General Foods, and the like. Every one of these companies was once a picture in someone's head.

But what happened?

They all took acute correlated action towards the pictures in their head. After a few cycles of time, they all experienced their early results.

Here's what's unique about result that take place stemming from a creator versus a creature. Creator results will always yield more results. Results are not only perpetual but expansive in nature. Results naturally produce additional results. With this, you have these same companies explode into industry giants over time. Not only are you meant to have a desire, then define and design that desire; you are meant to get results and those results will explode into more results. This all requires action.

Here are some strategies and reasons for motivated action.

1. Actions must point towards desired results.
2. You must be without excuses.
3. No action or low action produces low energy.
4. You do not want Regrets from not taking action.
5. Take Imperfect Action. No action is perfect. Move forward.
6. Take action in the face of what seems to be fear.
7. How you do anything is How you do everything. HYDA = HYDE

Be Rich in Results

Results have to be part of who you are. As I said, results automatically lead to the next level, but at that next level, you will receive more results. Then you must be consistent in getting results in the following areas.

1. Spiritual Results
2. Personal Results
3. Results in Your Relationships
4. Results in Your Business

Here's why it's important to get results in all of these areas. As I said in #7, how you do anything is how you do everything. Not getting results in one area will automatically lead to not getting results in all other areas. There must be a consistency at getting measurable results at all times. Your ability to obtain results lends to your credibility as a creator. Anything else, you're just a creature. A creature of habit.

How You Do Anything
Is How You Do Everything!

Allow me to make a point that might be a little on the edge. There's a reason why I listed spiritual results first. All results are spiritual. Personal results are spiritual. The results in your relationships are spiritual. Results in your business our spiritual. Remember, I said life is about results. To have an idea is to be like God, and to bring that idea to fruition is to do the things that God does. To produce something is a godly thing, because life does not happen without production. You are gifted in the space of the Creator to be a creator. So, creation is spiritual.

The idea of taking something that is not seen, and to bring it into the space of where it is seen and experienced is a spiritual work. That's why when results take place, it's like a seed; in that seed are many more results ready to go. The first commandment ever given was to be fruitful and multiply. Imagine that as a commandment. The order that is given to humans is to just not create results but create results on top of results. Let's take a look at personal results.

Most people don't take the time to contemplate how they want their life to turn out. For the most part, this is left up to outside forces and considerations. How awful is this. It's OK for people to live in this space of having their life designed for them, but this leaves one in the space have non-creation, therefore living a life where there is no life. This reminds me of the movie "The Walking Dead". When you take the time to design something that you desire for your future, then take the actions on that design, along with creating the right relationships around your vision, the results are for you to enjoy. In addition, you've become a witness to the capacity of the human being when it comes to the subject of accomplishment.

You must define and design the type of house you want, the type of car you would like to drive, and other things that you desire for your life that matches the greatness of who you are. When you take on the influence and design of others, and things happen, I wouldn't even call those results. Those are accidents. When you're not creating consistent results that are attributed to something that you thought of, life becomes a series of accidents. Anything that is not a mirror that reflects what's inside of you and does not match the intention or the direction of your purpose in life, you will experience a great deal of dead ends that you will run into that are injurious in nature.

Write the things down that you would like to happen for you, create the relationships that are equated to what you've written down, and then immediately move in that direction. Take action. Not only will you enjoy the results, your own results will begin to provide for you. This is a natural order of how things work in the Earth, therefore be "fruitful and multiply" is at the root of what life is.

Zero Excuses Keeps You Out of Poverty

Coming up with excuses is buying into your limitations. Now we live in a world where all things are naturally limited. An apple tree will always be an apple tree and produce apples. A lemon tree will always be a lemon tree and produce lemons. A cherry tree will always be a cherry tree and produce cherries. I'm sure you get the point. In addition, a horse will always produce other horses which will always do horse things. A cow will produce other cows which will always do cow things. A fruit fly will always produce other fruit flies which will always do fruit fly things. The same with the roach. The same with various types of cats. I'm sure you get the point.

All of life was designed with an endpoint in mind, so life is a perpetual system of limitation. The only thing that lives outside of limitation is your ability to think thoughts beyond any perceived limited existence. With that, there will be a natural tendency to be monolithic in your thinking and production, because that's what life expresses to us on the outside. Even when you think of a thought that is a beautiful creation, pretty quickly you can rethink that thing and have an excuse for not taking action. We do it all the time.

Brains are so intelligent; we can come up with the greatest excuses for not moving forward on something that we imagine that could be. Our concerns could be what others might think. Our concerns could be in our own ability to accomplish the idea that was set forth. It might seem natural to be distracted to doing something against the actions that we can take towards our greatest intention. In fact, it is unnatural.

Every time you make an evaluation or an assessment as to why you can't do something, that is an unnatural act. Yes, I said it, it is still an act. An excuse is an act or action. Sometimes the action that we take is to decide to not move forward for whatever reason. Excuses breed stagnation.

How do you overcome making excuses?

1. Stay in the energy space of being a creator.
2. Recognize the damaging effects that excuses cause.
3. After writing down a task or an idea, do something immediately towards that to generate the energy of it getting done.
4. Know that an excuse is an energy. This energy in motion will consistently work against you. Remember, that what you don't do is in motion also. Not doing is a creation.
5. Even if you made a verbal excuse, be mindful when you do, and immediately replace it with an actionable action. This takes away the "feeling" of an excuse.

Be Rich in Actions

Non-Action is not an option. Take it off the table. A body in motion stays in motion. This is based on Newton's first law of motion. Except in this case, not doing anything is still a form of motion. Instead of getting constant results, when you don't take action on what you want, non-achievement is still a result. But here's what you will find happening around you, because of the energy that you have set, so many other things in response will not get done. So, the mathematics applies to what you don't do as well as what you actually get done. You might as well take action and get things done.

The next fundamental part of action is consistency. All of your actions must match the direction of your intention. Most do not realize that there is a high cost to doing something different than your purpose and direction. Time spent on doing something else other than what you have set as an intention is time lost towards your intention. Now this might sound extremely simple, but it's something that people do not pay attention to. It all starts with the value that you put on what you desire versus the value of outside influences.

Outside environmental influences are an extreme reality. I will never discount the reality of the pressures that want to push you in a different direction, but you must pay attention to them. When we are distracted from our ultimate purpose, for the most part there's not a sense of loss of value. The direction that you move in consistently will tell the story of what you value. As a matter of fact, every move you make has a value and a cost. Here's a couple of things to keep in mind as you assess the actions that you take during the course of a day. I would advise you to monitor this day by day, and in some cases hour by hour.

1. Along with documenting something that comes to your imagination or your idea, immediately make a list of actions that you can take towards that. In addition, begin at least one or two of those actions immediately to establish the energy of direction. It only takes a moment to connect otherwise to something that has nothing to do with what you desire.

2. Make sure that every action written is consistent with your desire and direction. Do not be afraid to erase something when you feel that is not contributive to your desire.

3. Ask others to participate in the actions that you designate towards your purpose and destiny. Having others to work with you sets in a sense of accountability. This takes community.

4. Document when you complete something. Completing something that is directly tied to your purpose and intention we'll set the energy for doing the next thing. Here you are creating a cycle of getting things done that are consistent to where you're going.

5. When you find yourself off track, do not be afraid of reestablishing your direction.

The Perils of Regret

Regret is the form of language.

What!!!?

Yes, regret is a form of language. It is a system of information that will present itself as a result of you not taking action, or just simply didn't get something done, or did not get the results that you wanted. Have you ever had a great idea and you knew that you had a perfect idea. Then several years later you are watching TV and you see your idea on TV. You jump up and say that's my idea. The person that's now displaying what was once on your mind is now making millions of dollars on something that you thought of years earlier. That idea stayed in motion while you decided to stop. That's your regret speaking to you.

Remember, I said there's a cost to not taking action and then not getting the results you want. That cost has a voice and will speak back to you at some point in time. It is better to hear yourself now than to hear your regret later. If you don't do what comes to your mind and do things according to what you envision for yourself, somebody else will do it at some point in time.

It Is Better to Hear Yourself Now Than to Hear Your Regret Later!

You split energy and when you split your energy, meaning you come up with an idea and you don't act on that idea, you start with excuses; why it won't work, or it might not work, and what people will say, you're actually working against yourself. At this point you immediately split your energy, you are now working against yourself. Two different energies are working at the same time. You are speaking about the things that you want to do and then the other half of you is thinking about the reasons why you can't. This split energy causes stagnation.

Then stagnation becomes another energy that will speak directly back to you. Think of stagnant water.

What does stagnant water attract?

Yes, it attracts mosquitoes, bacteria, and other undesirables. Eventually stagnant water will begin to smell and stink. This layers on the problem of people not wanting to be around anything that's stagnant. It is here where you are creating an undesirable environment that communicates to you. This becomes the highest form of regret. Here are a few things that keep you out of the space of regret.

1. Place yourself around people who are action takers. Action takers are money makers. This is easily done by joining organizations that exist for this specific reason. This is the chief reason why my organization of rich friends is the optimum place to spend your time. You need to constantly and consistently hear what others are doing. Moreover, as you experience their accomplishments, it will set the rhythm of accomplishment within yourself.

2. Move from the energy of affirmations to the energy of afformations. Afformations is the energy that you pay attention to that others are doing, that becomes a reality within yourself. Practice doing versus practice saying. Don't affirm the language, afform the behavior.

3. Let what you do and what you get done be your motivator. Words are good, but what you do speaks louder not only to yourself, but it speaks to others. Your behavior is a rhythm that has a connotation of language attached to it.

4. If you ever get to the point where you regret something and that regret is clearly speaking to you, take that opportunity to do

something that speaks louder than your regret. Again, this is the power of your imagination and the power of your ideas. You can always move beyond regret by getting something done. As a matter of fact, words can't compete with regret. Only results can compete with regret.

Be Rich in Imperfect Action

Perfect action is the killer. Many people do not move unless they feel that things are perfectly in place in order to make a move. This leaves you exposed to external influences or environmental influences, wherein you must know that you have no control over. Something will always be out of place, and taking into consideration what's out of place before you make a start will keep you in a space of stagnation. I call it "analysis paralysis". Let your actions do your thinking for you.

Overthinking or the search for perfection is essentially just another excuse not to move. Some people are extremely proud of the fact that they can sit still and cover every base imaginable, not realizing that that's a behavior that is extremely damaging. A lot of work is done, yes, but there's been no movement or forward progression. It's like running on a treadmill, you're just as tired running on a treadmill than when you're running from point A to point B.

Here's the problem. Asking questions takes up time wherein you can be moving towards a specific destination. Moreover, you're usually the one that's asking the questions and coming up with a multiplicity of answers over and over again. That within itself becomes an activity, but it is an activity in futility.

Perfect action is a thing we're you are trying to be perfect and trying to make sure I got this right, or I got that right, the lighting must be perfect, do I have the logo, do I have the website, etc. All those things are really a lower conscious way of saying I don't think I can do this thing. Imperfect action causes you to get over perfectionism. You must be ok with getting it wrong. When it comes to the nature of action, getting it wrong is a valued way of getting to the point where you get it right. Movement carries more value than assessment.

In all actuality, perfection is selfish. This is when it becomes about you, and you only. It's not about who you're trying to serve. When I first started in real estate investing, I would go and I would look at what was out there, beating the streets. I would park my car and then I would walk a whole neighborhood looking for abandoned properties. They call it driving for dollars.

I was doing all those things that people I knew other people wouldn't do for sure. Somebody asked me on one of my videos you were professional, and you were a nurse, but now you out there looking crazy in the streets.

Why?

I said, I don't care what it looks like to you, but this is something that I don't think that I have to do, I must do it. When I got started, I was doing all the things that so many other people wouldn't. I was doing foolish things of the world to confound the wise. Action to me was vital.

Starting and then doing will get you there. Not doing anything will never get you there. Be careful when "getting it right" becomes an excuse. You must recognize at any given point where this is an excuse versus a reality.

Is Fear Real?

What we consider to be fear is simply a chemical in your body where what we define as fear or call fear is associated with. This chemical is called adrenaline or epinephrine. It's a chemical that's produced by the adrenal glands. Fear is a false prediction or a wrong idea.

What do I mean by this?

In order to feel fear, this chemical has to be released and present in your body. This chemical is a response to something in front of you. Most scientists call it "fight or flight". This is where a chemical is released in response to something that is considered to be dangerous.

Do you stay and fight the danger, or do you run away from the danger?

Here's what's been discovered about adrenaline or epinephrine, or the chemical that we call fear. This fear is also displayed as anxiety. Essentially, fear and anxiety are the exact same things, but it is not fear, nor anxiety. It's just a group of molecules. When this chemical is present, the assignment is to stay in fight or run, but in actuality adrenaline carries the education to defeat whatever danger that's in front of you. The presence of adrenaline is assigned to move forward. This is the truth about adrenaline. Adrenaline is present to eliminate the question and not to pose a question. Just move forward, or it's time to move forward. This is the messaging of this molecular group. Let me give you an example.

If a 9-foot grizzly bear stands in front of you and roars with all of its might, the tendency is to run away. But let that same 9-foot grizzly bear stand over a small baby in a baby's carriage. In this case, the mother standing three feet away is not making a choice in the matter, she's going after the bear, no questions asked. The question is eliminated. The bear is on the run. Somehow the mother knew exactly what to do to eliminate the threat. This is the assignment of adrenaline. It's not "fight or flight", it is move beyond. There is no such thing as fear, only the presentation of the information to move beyond the presentation.

In reality, adrenaline is present at every decision that you have to make, especially those decisions that are launched from the imagination or your idea. Imagination and ideas will always activate adrenaline, but this adrenaline is misread as fear, or a point where you think you have to make a choice of standing still, running away, or moving forward. Adrenaline is made for moving forward.

Why?

Adrenaline comes as a result of your adrenal gland converting your idea or the space of your imagination into sugar. This is your body acting towards the dream that you set as an intention. Your body forms adrenaline and releases adrenaline in response to the adrenal gland converting what you said as an intention into sugar. This is a very powerful reality. But we are taught that this is the space of fear, and we have questions to ask at this point. No, you don't. Adrenaline means to move forward.

Like a GPS on a cell phone, adrenaline maps out the direction of your intention. It is simply saying that you know how to get this thing done, so move forward. To take in consideration of whether you should move forward or not is simply splitting your energy, and as you know, a split energy causes stagnation.

Your cells in your body are listening for the energy of your progression. When adrenaline is released from your adrenal gland, it travels to your blood cells. Without going into great detail, your blood cells then records the message that comes from the adrenal gland that carries the memory of the future that you have defined and designated. This is a very powerful reality.

The very cells in your body are listening to your ideas and responding to your imagination. We've been falsely told that the anxiety that we feel is the space where we ask questions, but to properly use the chemical formula of adrenaline, means that you move forward with confidence. Adrenaline is releasing the language that the memory of what you want is now complete. Not only is it complete, you now know how to get to where you're going. Adrenaline is a matter of trust, moreover, trust in yourself. This is how the early greats of the industrial age and information age accomplished great feats without an education. They just knew how to get it done. This includes Henry Ford, Marjorie Post, the Wright Brothers, John Morgan, Steve Jobs, Sam Walton, Jeff Bezos and many others who got things done without the benefit of knowing exactly how to get them done.

They took imperfect action. They had great ideas and their compelling imagination caused them to move on what they saw. This information was stored and memorized in their body. Moreover, this information was stored in awaiting cells within their body that were listening for their greatness. They then knew how to get it done and took action. The formula remains the same for you.

As a matter of fact, these great inventors and leaders of the great industrial age were all in an organization led by Napoleon Hill. This organization was the foundation that created the energy for innovation. This is why I said you must get around people who think like you think and have visions on the level of your vision. They were all rich friends consistently meeting in different parts of the country to discuss their progressions. Their organization was exclusive and was steeped in intent.

We should all be modern day rich friends. I always say, how you do anything is how you do everything. In addition, how you do everything is how people respond to you. This powerful group was responsive to each other and their respective ideas. You need people around you that can correctly respond to who you are and respond to the height of your imagination. This makes an extreme difference in how you move forward, and an extreme difference in the actions that you take. Being part of an exclusive organization where high intention is the natural order carries an extreme value.

Ask yourself the following questions.

1. What actions are you taking towards your dream?
2. Then who are the quality people that surround the actions that you take?
3. Who responds correctly to the actions that you take?
4. Who values the actions that you take?
5. More importantly, who can speak the right things into you that push you towards correct action?

6. Who can you model your actions after, wherein you have access to?

7. Then who is acting correctly towards the actions that you're taking?

This is the value of being in an organization that systematically drives you in the right direction. We must all be rich friends.

7 *Reflect the Rich*

Reflection is a vital part of life. There are several spaces that you can reflect on and should reflect on. The first is self-reflection our self-evaluation. The next space of reflection is reflecting on the results within life. And then there's the space of reflection that involves place. What I mean by this is you have to always reflect on where you are. Let's list these out.

1. Self-reflection.
2. Reflection on your results.
3. You must reflect on where you are, or the place of reflection.

You Must Be Rich in Understanding Who You Are

When I talk about reflection, I mean just that. Reflection denotes a mirrored event. How do things mirror from you? To answer that question, you must start with you.

Why is this important?

Everything that you do has an impact on people. Moreover, everything that you have has an impact on other people. In life, you must determine what your impact will be on other people. In addition, you must determine what impact you would want to have in this world.

Of course, we're talking about purpose, but your purpose cannot arise without your imagination and your ideas.

When addressing the question of reflection, as your ideas go out from who you are, your ideas are reflective of who you are. Of course, you know that your imagination is the direct reflection of who you are. With this, you must take stock and who you are. Again, you start with value and appreciation. Anything that you are or determine yourself to be is a transferable commodity to other people. You must determine how you will show up in the world. This is done by definition and design. The impact of value that you have determined for yourself on others is extremely acute. Just by meeting people you build an instant relationship whether you like it or not. You become an immediate stored memory in somebody else's body even if they only saw you for a few seconds.

A lot can be said in a few seconds. If a picture can speak 1000 words, imagine what your presence can do. So, you must pre plan your presence to have optimal impact everywhere you go.

Preplan and Practice Your Presence

When it comes to reflection, the first reflection is how you see yourself. The second reflection is how other people see you, moreover, how other people are impacted by you. You must know your level of impact with full intention of impacting people that you meet. Literally, you leave them something to remember about you. Here are some personal characteristics that you must have in your bag of impact.

Loyalty

Honesty

Integrity

Family

Security

Wealthy

Legacy

These are a few things that I hold as a standard, with the understanding that this is who I am towards other people. As an example, as to how you can show up, when I show up, I like for people to get a sense of loyalty from me. I like for people to experience my honesty. I would like people to know my integrity. I would like people to understand that I'm very family oriented. With this I want them to get a good sense that connecting with me will give them a strong sense of family. I like for people to feel secure around me. Moreover, I want people to wake up to their sense of wealth when they experience the presence of my wealth. And then everything that I do is to leave a legacy.

When it comes to business, you're in business to make money. That's for sure. But you can't be in business to make sales.

What do I mean by that?

Don't you have to make sales to make money?

Making sales shouldn't be something that you do, because sales come as a result based on how a person feels. Sales should be a natural result that comes from a person having a great feeling about who you are and what you have to offer. A good businessperson concentrates on how a person feels when they are around them.

Even with this, how you come across to others must be extremely authentic. In Orlando FL, and Los Angeles CA you have a great amount of theme parks, such as Disney World, Universal Studios, and SeaWorld.

These companies take on billions of dollars a year. Why? They are the experts at influencing people's feelings. People don't go to theme parks because they want to buy tickets, people go to theme parks to gain particular feelings. Not only do the parks have a lot of rides that invoke extreme emotions, but they also fill the park with the music and smells that are causing you to feel a certain way as you move throughout the park. Once in a theme park food is three to four times more than what you would purchase at a restaurant or a grocery store, but people don't mind spending that money because they're technically caught up in their feelings.

What you must realize is that most companies that are doing extremely well, let's say the top ten companies in the world, actually don't sell you anything, they are the experts at making you feel a certain way. As we discussed in the earlier chapter, Apple Inc not only makes you feel really good about the products that you buy, but they also make you feel really good about the packaging. When you walk into a grocery store, the promotions are a part of why you might be there, but the store is set up to cause you to feel a certain way while you're there. Have you ever gone into a grocery store to buy one thing, and then come out with a whole basket full of groceries?

This is because they impacted your feelings and did not have to sell you anything. You bought all of that stuff based on how you felt. Have you noticed that grocery stores do not have salespeople to show you the bread, salespeople to point out how good the meat is. No, you just buy because they spent a lot of money on impacting your feelings with the lighting, the colors, the smells, and the music playing in the background. With all of this, they are influencing people's movements. To put it in a scientific way, they work hard to impact your nervous system, so you automatically buy things without coercion.

One of the best strategies for business is to not concentrate on building clientele, but building relationships. People might stop for a minute to listen to a sales pitch, but when you actually connect with the person, but moreover do it genuinely, people will spend money in the context of that relationship. A relationship that leads to a feeling is much more influential than a sales pitch, wherein you're trying to get a person to buy something from you. This is why you have to practice your presentation. Focus on how you make a person feel.

When you are impacting the emotions, you are literally impacting the flow of hormones within a person's body. All hormones will find their receptors that are attached to cells within the body, because hormones communicate with those cells. Literally, your authenticity determines the movements in someone else's body. I display the experience of;

Loyalty

Honesty

Integrity

Family

Security

Being Wealthy

Legacy

Therefore, a person will gain the feeling of the same.

Think of yourself as a theme park in a way.

What experience do you cause a person to have when they are around you?

How do people feel when they leave your presence?

What do people gain from connecting with you?

When people leave your presence, they should naturally feel an increase in their personal value.

Why do some stores go out of their way, more specifically department stores, to have their store display extreme elegance and wealth?

Because that is how they want you to feel when you're in their store. Then when they feel that way, they will naturally want to participate by buying, so they can take the feeling of wealth with them. Most of the time they do not really care about the cost. They want to simply take the experience that they gained in the store that led to a feeling back to their house.

I'm going to be purposefully redundant here to make a point. Loyalty invokes a feeling. People would like to feel that you're not going to switch up on them or take something away from them through betrayal. Honesty invokes a feeling. People feel better when there's a sense of trust. Integrity invokes a feeling. People like to feel that you are following through on a promise. The sense of family invokes a feeling. People like to feel that they belong to something. A sense of being wealthy invokes a feeling. People like to feel that they have something and that they are worth something. A sense of security invokes a feeling.

People like to feel protected. A sense of legacy invokes a feeling. People like to feel that something good is going to last long. That's the purpose of establishing a sense of legacy.

With my circle of rich friends, these are the feelings that I desire for them to have within this community, but I have to be that first, because my circle of rich friends' community is a reflection of the values that I must personally carry. Here are a few things you can do to establish what is reflected from through self-reflection.

1. Make a list of personal values that you feel will impact others.
2. Preplan your values. Why is this? You might sit down and through self-reflection list values that you want to be known for, but those values have to show up as you interact with others. Remember as a child when your mother took you to the grocery store? Before you went in, she would set all the rules of your behavior while you're in that grocery store. Don't touch this, don't touch that, don't ask for anything, and don't cut up while you're in the store. That was your mother pre-planning the values. Sometimes you have to sit and tell yourself how you're going to act towards people, or it can easily slip your mind what your intentions are.
3. Practice those values. Because of external considerations, like events beyond your control, circumstances that happen, and other environmental influences, you might not realize how easy it is to be taken off point from your personal values. Sometimes what you are reflecting towards somebody else is a result of something that happened to you. So, you must consciously be aware of your values at all times.

4. Pay attention to the growth of your connections, both the girls within that connection and the growth in the number of connections that you have. You are establishing a reason for people to be around you because of who you are.

5. Self-reflection becomes your reflection, and it will show up in the feelings of the people that are around you.

Reflection in Your Results

One of the greatest spaces of reflection is what shows up in your results. What shows up in your results is reflective of who you are. This is why achievement is important. Your achievements are simply a picture of who you are that is an outer reflection. A lot of times when people diminish the importance of achievement, that within itself is a reflection of that person. It is sad when people of that nature attempt to make non-achievement or little achievement a personal value that they would then in turn teach others. But in reality, non-achievement is still an achievement.

The results that you obtain in life tells a story. First, it tells the story of who you are. Secondly, that story has an impact on other individuals. You must be concerned about the impact that you have on others through your personal presence, but in addition, you have to pay attention to the impact that your results have on others. This is also a reflection.

When you plant a tree, let's say an apple tree, a seed goes in the ground and through a series of growth points, including germination, growing roots, piercing the ground, growing the body of the tree, and then the leaves, finally the fruit. What you are seeing is not just the process of a plant growing into a tree and producing fruit, you are witnessing a series of reflections. The fruit in the end reflects what was in the seed. All of life works this way, including yours.

Everything in life bears a result. That result becomes evidence of a purpose. For the most part, most fruit trees look alike before they bear fruit. In some cases, like the cherry tree, blooms will appear as a sign that the fruit is on its way. It is then that you can tell what type of tree it is. It is the blooms and the fruit that signified purpose. You can establish a purpose for your life, but purpose is not known without achievement. Purpose is not known without reaching results. You are the seed, and your accomplishments are a reflection of what's in you.

I cannot express this enough. Never devalue your imagination or the ideas that you might come up with. That value must be held in the seed which is you. The only way that people can witness your purpose which is a reflection of who you are, you have to accomplish that idea. Accomplished ideas become the influence that will very well influence and drive the space of somebody else's accomplishment. Your achievements will become the inspiration for somebody else to achieve.

This is an extreme space of reflection. Not only are you reflecting what's in you by creating something outside of yourself, that creation becomes a reflection in somebody else. You are essentially dealing with a system of mirrors. If you have children, this point becomes even more vital. Children become what they see, and without you having an achievement-oriented mind, children will be influenced by other things that they witness in life outside of you. You should have the biggest impact on your children. When they don't see their parents achieving, they find the next closest thing to them to learn from.

Not only are your children a biological reflection of who you are, they also will reflect your ability to achieve. This level of influence also goes beyond your children. If you own a business, you will want your employees to reflect the values that you set for yourself. If those values are not preplanned and practiced, your employees we'll bring the influence of somebody else's energy into your business. You must be the biggest influence when it comes to people within your circle. Otherwise, you'll have competing energies.

A mother or father with an unruly child is most likely not dealing with a child that intends to be unruly, but that parent is competing with an energy that a child has picked up from somebody else. Now there's a competing energy. This is because the parent has not established influence. The only way that you can establish influence is through results that reflect the greatest parts of who you are. Yes, you can command a child to do something as a parent, but what a child learns from a parent that sets an example of greatness, that's a reflection into that child that other outside influences cannot compete with.

Your Idea = The Achievement of the Idea

Achievement is a reflection, and without it, there is no system of measurement for who you are. Do not be afraid of this notion. A lot of people are afraid to achieve.

Why?

Because their achievement becomes offensive to people that they care about or close to them. Not everybody has the capacity to generate an idea through the imagination, if they do, they do not possess the ability or talent to achieve that idea. With those types of people, your achievement will offend them. What's sad is that that becomes the motivation to not do something or to not achieve. You cannot be worried about somebody not liking you because you are achievement oriented.

Be rich in your results. And don't fear your results. A lot of times when anxiety pops up when you are trying to move forward, it is not that you have an anxiety towards where you're going, that anxiety is launched against the people around you that don't carry the same energy. When you are beginning to outgrow somebody, your anxiety is painting the difference between you and that person. It has nothing to do with whether you can accomplish what you desire to accomplish or not. Life is not so much about where you're going than it is about where you are leaving from.

The Determination of Place

This point of reflection is probably the most important of the three, although all of them carry an extreme value. All of your places must reflect who you are. This is something that many don't put a lot of thought to, or they really don't see it as being important or a point of value.

What I mean by place is just that. What are the places that you put yourself in that's like you?

This is definitely something that you have to take measurement in and take stock in. The places that you're in you must reflect who you are.

Why?

You are dealing with energy. Along with energy you are dealing with influence, meaning that energy will always influence. A place doesn't have to be a physical space, but it could also mean the people that you place around you, it could mean the place in space of consciousness that you decide to be in, and it could mean a place of ideology.

If I should ask, where are you?

Anything that can be an answer to that particular question is a place. When you deal with places and energy, you must be aware at all times the impact that a place will have on your body first and foremost. Then you must manage the impact of that place on your future. This is something that people usually will not regard.

Place has a connotation of sound, because even though you don't hear it, a place will speak to you, and we'll speak to who you are. You just can't go into any place, moreover you can't go into any home, or a particular business as far as that's concerned. Energy is always at work, which means influence is always at work. Places are contributive to the space in which you make a determination towards your future. The power of this is that you can choose the places you decide to be. Let's first take your home.

Oprah Winfrey always says that your home must give rise to you and who you are. Your home must speak to who you are and where you're going at all times. She said the pictures on your wall must speak to the direction that you're going and speak to your intention for your life. Your home must show your purpose. The colors, the type of fabric, the way things are arranged, and the like, all of it must tell the same story. She said that if anything is broken in your home, you either fix it or get rid of it. A broken clock, a broken toaster, or a broken TV. Whatever it is, you must make it a point to get rid of those things, because the brokenness of those things will speak to you.

Buy pictures and artwork that says something to you about the future that you have designed. Your home becomes the perfect opportunity to set the energy that's more consistent with who you are. As I said in the other chapter, I imagined my vacation, and then essentially took my home and made it into a vacation spot. So, every day that I'm at home, I'm literally on vacation. The sounds are the music in your home should be songs that are aligned with your intention and purpose. Again, we are talking about what's reflected from you.

A lot of times we aren't successful in life, because we surround ourselves in our close spaces with things that don't match our greatness. As I said earlier, how you do anything is how you do everything. Don't expect to be successful in business without starting with that same success in your own home.

To drive the point, be very particular about where you go shopping. Those places must reflect who you are and your intentions. Go to the better stores even if you have to pay more money. The reason being is that a store owner that places a high value in their customers will take the time to create a place in space that leads to encouragement and invokes feelings that we had spoken about earlier. If you go to stores where the floors aren't cleaned, things aren't organized, there's little or no customer service, dimly lighted, there's no dress code for the employees; when you walk into those places and spaces, that speaks to the value that you have placed in yourself because you feel the need to be around something or somewhere that doesn't express your values.

The same goes for places of entertainment. There is nothing wrong with having a great time wherever you're going and spending money for that great time. But what are those places offering that speak to who you are. All of these are a matter of reflection, a definite reflection on what you think about yourself. There are certain neighborhoods that I don't drive in, because I need to take the time to drive in the spaces and places where I see myself going. I'm sure all of this makes sense to you now.

Add to this list religious organizations, clubs, and the like.

Do they reflect the values of your future?

If not, find better places to be. If you went into a hospital and saw dirty floors, beds are not made-up, stains on the bed, the nurses are dressed in street clothes, and there was leftover food all over the place, you would say come and Get Me Out of Here! Not only will a place reflect the condition of who you are, but the conditions of places can also be reflected back to you and then you become that. You must value the places that you're in.

Be the Place to Be

The next phase of this type of reflection when it comes to place, it is the energy of your personal space that becomes the place for others. I've touched on this a little bit before; you should be the biggest influence within your space. You become what others want to be. And if you are an authentic person, the value of who you are will quickly be reflected in others. You become the place to be.

My circle of rich friends, which is a community that I have personally developed, is an example of a place to be. First it reflects my personal values, whereas the people who join will have my personal values reflected on to them.

Loyalty

Honesty

Integrity

Family

Security

Being Wealthy

Legacy

The same goes for you, you must reflect the values that you hold dear constantly and consistently, because you become the place that will influence and impact others. I can't express enough the fact that who you are should invoke a feeling into someone else. This mode of existence is reflective in nature. What are you reflecting? Because I measure and monitor my reflection, the community that I built of rich friends reflects the same values.

Then my intention for my circle of rich friends is to impact a feeling within a person's body that will naturally cause them to be better. Here are some elements that you will feel by being in a place that contributes to who you are.

1. You'll get a great sense that you have finally found the place to be. This is where you'll gain a great sense of integrity.

2. You will get a great sense that this is a safe environment to learn in.

3. You will know that this is a place where you can grow.

4. You will get a great sense that you're in a place where you can open up and be honest about what you want to accomplish, and then know that people will respond correctly to you because it is a designated place of accomplishment. This is where you will gain a great sense of honesty.

5. You will find that the energy of others within the community matches your energy. This is where you would gain a great sense of family.

6. In this place you will witness winning. By being in a circle of friends that are winners, that energy will be reflected into you which will naturally upgrade your sense of winning. This is where you will gain a great sense of being wealthy.

7. This is where you would gain a great sense of accomplishment, because other people are there to celebrate your wins. This creates the foundation for winning repeatedly. This is where you will gain a great sense of legacy.

Your reflection carries value. Not only must you be concerned about the spaces of reflection that extends from you, but be in the places that correctly reflect who you are. I used the word wealthy earlier, which is the perfect word to explain what I mean by reflecting out. A person's wealth is not something that they accomplish, it is something that they reflect. You do not gain wealth, you reflect wealth.

If you drive under some of the underpasses in Los Angeles, you'll see a whole lot of homeless people. Downtown Los Angeles, there's literally a city of homeless people. If you watch this on the news or any other documentary that's pointing out the homeless problem in Los

Angeles, that is the exact language that they use; there is a homeless problem or a homeless crisis. But not really. What you're looking at when you see a homeless camp, it's not homelessness at all but a question of capacity. You are looking at a capacity of mindset, then the living conditions that reflect that mindset. To most of those people, they are in a perfect space. They don't see homelessness.

Now there are some that are out there that want to be in a different place in space and ended up there through a series of tragedies. But very few mind you. Most of them love where they are, and it's a reflection of their intention or the level of their intention for life. They might not feel like designing a great life, or chase after some of the things and values that other people go for. They are comfortable where they're at. Somebody in a different place might look at them and say, this is horrible. It is only horrible to that person who doesn't see what the homeless person sees. A place of comfort.

On the opposite end of that you can go into the wealthiest neighborhoods, and you would say based on what you see that this is a wealthy neighborhood. What you're looking at is not wealth, but what you're looking at is capacity. Everything that you see no matter where a person lands on the spectrum, is simply a point of reflection of what's in that person. The good news is that you don't have to work to create something great outside of you. All you have to do is create that on the inside through your imagination and through your ability to create an idea, and then reflect that on the outside.

Essentially once you've driven your imagination to the highest points possible, and then have the intelligence to place yourself around those who have the same capacity, those persons will reflect into you what you need to get to where they are. This is the power of place. This is the power of reflection.

Be rich in what you see in yourself.

8 *Have a Rich Community*

Achievement, accomplishment, success, and winning are a natural part of life. Evidently, due to the fact that you have obtained this book and are reading the content, it must be important to you that these terms are evident in your life. My desire is to serve that space of desire that you hold dear. It is my mission in life to provide the absolute best solutions to anything that might impede your progress. And the key to achievement, accomplishment, success, and winning in life is progress.

What do I mean by progress?

Forward movement, but forward movement, wherein each point of movement there is expansion. This must be noted because you can have forward movement, wherein each point measured within forward movement, there is no expansion or growth. This has been the experience of most of the population. Getting ahead, but not getting ahead. The work has been put in. The effort has been put in. The time has been put in. Moreover, the money has been put in, but there has been no growth. Achievement has been distant and allusive.

You bought all the programs. Attended all the seminars. Took all the classes. Read all the books. Went through all the courses, but you haven't quite locked into the thing that really works. You see it work for a select few, so you try harder. Still, something is missing, but you can't quite put your finger on it.

I became a nurse because my passion in life is to serve people. To see them better. My nursing career provided that. But at some point, that wasn't enough. I overcame incredible odds to get to where I am now, so this has to be something that anyone can do, achieve, or to accomplish anything that comes to their minds. As a nurse, quite obviously, I was working on bodies all day every day. My mission was to restore health. Well at some point, a body would end up in a state of not being healthy. We are talking about a disease or some type of injury. Disease and injury are not a natural state of the body. In either case, restoration had to take place. This was the goal every time.

Allow me to state this as a case. When you are not achieving, not accomplishing, not successful, and not winning, you are not in a state of health. This is the way you must see it. These things fall into the same space as disease and injury. How do you handle disease and injury? You must move from the state of disease and injury to a state of health. If you broke your leg, you do not take a seminar on "how to fix a leg". If you had a heart attack, if you stop to read a book on heart attacks, you will be dead. If you had a terminal disease like cancer, you do not take a class to study cancer and get certified as a cancer expert.

In all of these things, whether it be a disease or injury, you put yourself in a place where the people who are trained to restore your health can do just that; restore your health.

Achievement, accomplishment, success, and winning is not a matter of "how to", it is a matter of "where to". Think of the subject of achievement as a state of being or a state of health. Think of accomplishment as a state of being or a state of health. Think of success as a state of being or a state of health. Think of winning as a state of being or a state of health. When you find yourself not in that correct state, you go to a place wherein you can be restored to this natural state of achievement, accomplishment, success, and winning. Someone that has been trained has to work on you. Most people pay big money to learn and work towards, wherein they actually need to be worked on.

This is a value that is not counted when it comes to the subject of success. It is also the reason why you see so few people winning while most others struggle, fight, survive, and yes, even lose. In those spaces it seems that the struggling, the fighting, the surviving, and losing is perpetual in nature. Even those who reach some level of what they believe to be successful, they are stuck and can't move forward or break past a barrier. This condition is a matter of health, not a matter of something you must get over or get past. To put it bluntly, when you can't win, you are sick.

The Source of Optimal Health

I will address this by addressing the misconception. We don't have a problem, just a misconception. It is now a known scientific fact that 85% of all diseases come as a result of stress. Except in the case of injury, all stress comes from relationships and money issues, and those two or irrevocably tied together. Making money is a matter of relationship because money is garnered on the basis of exchange that invokes a flow. This flow is a natural state of health. Being wealthy is a natural state of health.

All else is some form of stress in one form or another. When you do not have a vision, dream, or an intention for a great future, you leave your body in a state of stress. When there is not a deep abiding love, wherein that energy is turned towards your vision, dream, and intention for a great future for yourself, your body is in a state of stress. Then when you are not experiencing the wealth or flow from the interaction of your future consciousness with a consciousness directed towards you, your body is in a state of stress.

There's a book called CURE by M. Robbins. In it he describes a car accident and the injuries that come as a result leave the body in a state of stress. But stress as a result of someone hurting you based on words and behavior towards you is more dangerous than the stress resulting from a car accident. Lack of attention, a lack of agreement, lack of acknowledgement, lack of availability, and the like. All of these are damaging energies that contribute to the inability to be successful or to reach a point of achievement. The source of health comes from defining and designing a specific desire towards your future, and then having those who are close to you to give you attention, be in agreement with you, acknowledge your greatness, and then make themselves available to you through their actions. Any other condition is not a state of health.

The Vitalness of Connection

Generally, as a nurse, when people come in with either a serious disease or a serious injury, they are assessed and immediately connected to vital fluids that will assist in their recovery. They're also connected to a series of machines that measure their heart rate, their oxygen rate, and other important biophysical factors that are important to their recovery.

There is absolutely nothing wrong with books, seminars, classes, trainings, certification programs, and the like when you know that you're not achieving the desired things that you want in life. But what is really needed is that you would have to place yourself into a space where you have the connections that's bringing you back to a natural state of health. Some would say attend this seminar to learn how to win. I would say connect with something and somebody that is winning. Some would say take a class on how to accomplish your desires. That's all well and good. But I say, place yourself in the space where you're connected to the energies that provide you with the vital resources that you need to recover.

Then you need the right connections that can properly monitor the state of your body, so you can properly receive what you need to return to health. Achievement, accomplishment, success, and winning are about connection after you established the direction that you want to go in. Thirdly, you need competent people around you that are educated and trained to restore health. You need a group of people that can attend to your unhealthy condition. These are the nurses, the doctors, the physician assistance, the orderlies, etc. Besides your connections you are acutely attended to bring you back to health. This takes a community and an organization.

Not achieving is a condition. Not accomplishing is a condition. Not being successful is a condition. Not winning is a condition. To change the condition, you need the connections, you need the proper monitoring, and you need personnel that is capable of attending to your condition. Put yourself in the spaces and places where that community can serve the optimal state that you desire to be in. The state of your health is achieving your imagination and the ideas you set forth. The source of your health is the community that is built around the space of your greatness.

In my personal life, I myself have joined the necessary communities that lead me to my higher spaces of achievement and accomplishment. You must ask yourself the question, where is the community that contributes to my health? As a nurse, I know very well the importance of having people present that will optimize your condition.

Pay Attention to The Connections That Are Contributing Energies to Your Choices!

Be rich in community.

Value Your Spaces

I cannot even begin to overemphasize the value of space. Once again, I attribute this value to my grandmother, because I was able to move out of the space of extreme criticism and evaluation into a space where someone recognized my greatness and agreed with my greatness. My grandmother played a major role in reconstituting my understanding of what possibility was. A great community will adjust the constitution of your understanding. This is where you gain the health of achievement and the health of accomplishment.

A Great Community Will Adjust the Constitution of Your Understanding.

There are energies that lead to being in an optimum space of success. Let me remind you of what the elements are. Please understand that these elements constitute a system that will ultimately guarantee you're winning in life.

1. Define, design, determine, and develop your desire.

2. Build the correct relationships around that exact desire. The building of these connections must have an exclusive nature about it. Your relationships become the first space of place.

3. Once in the context of great connections growth will happen. You must monitor and measure your growth. If there is no growth, change the connections.

4. Now you must reach a finishing point. Reality doesn't exist until the fruit becomes available. Remember, it is the fruit that states your purpose. You can talk about purpose, but purpose is not realized without results.

5. You must be a master of your own imagination. Prioritize the ideas that come to your head. This is an energy that is the beginning of your purpose. Ideas rest in the ground of who you are as a seed that is meant to be published and produced outside of yourself. Without ideas, there are no results. You'll just live the results designed by others. Value your ideas.

6. Take acute and accurate action towards your imagination. You cannot desire one thing, and then act towards another thing.

7. Now place yourself in a community that reflects who you are, which will enable you to reflect who you are outside of who you are. A tree is known by the fruited bears. Place yourself in the orchard of accomplishment. When you are around people who are successful, it drives the success in you.

8. Now regenerate the process all over again.

The eight energies that I'm sharing with you are not arbitrary in the least. Every energy is biophysically aligned with your body. Earlier in the book I've mentioned on several occasions the power of your body, and how it contributes to assisting you to accomplish something that you set as a vision in your life or an intention for your life. In the Bible it says that you are fearfully and wonderfully made. This is almost an understatement. The privilege of imagination is huge, because it allows you to drive past any circumstances that is undesirable by simply building a desire beyond the circumstances. No animal can do this.

What you don't want is to have a systemic existence of a desire, that means greatness keeps poking at you. It doesn't stop. You know you're supposed to be in a better place. You know you're supposed to be accomplishing greater things. You know that you're supposed to be living your purpose. You know you're supposed to have more money than you have right now. You know you're supposed to have resources to support the people that you love. You have a great sense that there's something more. Do not allow this to be the case while sitting in a stagnant space.

Use the system above to activate your body, because when I say this is a matter of health, I'm not saying this as an allegory. When you are not in this space of your greatest potential, your body will suffer disease. As a matter of fact, as I mentioned earlier, your cells are listening for information that pertains to your destination. When you are incapable of visualizing yourself in great spaces, your body experiences damage. To be very specific, you will naturally lose magnesium and copper. This draws down the production of energy within your cells. This simply means you cannot afford to not dream. Moreover, it means you cannot afford to not accomplish those dreams.

Not only does your body respond when you have a vision, but when you don't have a vision, your body still responds. This is the nature of who you are. To put it in the simplest terms, you have 7 glands that release hormones. Each stage of the system that I just shared with you, when you practice each of those seven things, hormones are released from corresponding glands within your body. Life is about release. Life is about what comes from you. You are designed to release what you imagine into the world. Even when a pregnant woman births a child, that is an example of release. Everything that comes from you is aligned with giving birth. Because your ideas are a seed to something that will essentially be produced at some point.

When your body is not processing a future, the communication amongst the glands are stagnated, because the releases that are to come from those glands are inhibited. Let me remind you, you are designed biophysically to accomplish things. You are designed by your biophysically for achievement. You are designed biophysically to be successful. You're designed biophysically to win. Why are so many people sick today? Why do so many people have diabetes today? Why are pharmaceutical companies so rich? Because we medicate the space that has been diminished due to lack of vision. People do not know how to dream.

Here's my overall principles that will not only drive you to the space of your desire, but following this methodology will make it perpetually expansive. This is the methodology that you will experience in My Rich Friends Circle.

Create

Learn how to develop a strong financial foundation, set clear financial goals, and create a roadmap to achieve your designated space. The Elegance of Earning must be your focus.

Connect

Connecting to your framework can emphasize the importance of building relationships, establishing networks, and fostering meaningful connections with others. This can apply to various aspects of life, whether it's forming alliances in a strategic sense, building a supportive community, or enhancing personal and professional relationships to achieve your goals.

Control

Discover how to effectively manage your finances, track your progress, and make informed decisions that lead to financial success so that everything you do becomes easy. This is an art.

Conquer

Begin to master the art of your respective choice for your future, and scale that business or career to new heights, ensuring long-term financial growth and stability.

To create, connect, control, and conquer establishes culture. I will show how to arrange the energies of winning under these master principles.

To Create, Connect, Control, And Conquer Establishes Culture.

Here's a cross reference of this book with My Rich Friends Circle

Create

Chapter 1 – Start at the highest space of your value.
Chapter 5 – Generate great ideas through your imagination.

Connect

Chapter 2 – Relate to others according to your imagination and ideas.
Chapter 6 – Take the necessary actions that are aligned with your ideas. Monitor actions towards you.

Control

Chapter 3 – Measure and Monitored your growth.
Chapter 7 – Reflect on where you are at.

Conquer

Chapter 4 – Finish what you start.
Chapter 8 – Regenerate your success on another level.

These are the principles that I share with my rich circle of friends. These are the principles that are shared back with me within my circle of rich friends. You're never in this space where life is forcing you to not get done what you want to get done as far as your desire is concerned. You can create, you can connect, you can control, and you definitely can conquer. Creating the space of accomplishing what you desire is found in the place where you decide to be, and then the connections that you decide to make. This is the foundation of reaching the point of experiencing the life you want.

We should all be rich friends.

My Offer to You

Unlock the Power of Abundance: Join the Rich Friends Circle!

Dear Friend,

Allow me to share a captivating story with you—a tale of resilience, growth, and unwavering determination. It's a story that led to the creation of something truly extraordinary—the Rich Friends Circle—an empowering community of women like you, who are destined for greatness in every aspect of life.

Once upon a time, there was a remarkable woman named Tasha McCray. Her journey was filled with twists and turns, but one thing remained constant: her unwavering desire for abundance, not just in wealth but in every beautiful facet of life. From being a teenage parent at thirteen to becoming a multi-talented entrepreneur, real estate investor, and Amazon best-selling author, Tasha's life was a testament to the power of a determined heart.

Through her incredible experiences, Tasha realized that true success isn't merely about working harder, but about working smarter. Building a fulfilling life requires the right mindset, solid money management, and the power of community and connection.

And so, the Rich Friends Circle was born—a safe haven for like-minded women entrepreneurs and professionals, all determined to unlock their fullest potential and embrace a life of abundance, joy, and purpose. Together, we uplift, support, and inspire each other, sharing insights, strategies, and celebrations as we navigate our paths to success.

NOW IT'S YOUR TURN

Today, I invite you to join our exclusive Rich Friends Circle—a community that will elevate your journey and redefine your possibilities. As a member, you'll gain access to:

Tailored Insights: Benefit from Tasha's wisdom and experiences, honed from a lifetime of entrepreneurial endeavors, nursing, and real estate expertise. Learn to build proper systems that lead to growth and prosperity.

Empowering Connections: Connect with a group of ambitious women who share your vision and passion. Celebrate each other's victories and support one another through challenges.

Exclusive Content: Access to exclusive content, webinars, and workshops designed to help you thrive in your personal and professional life.

Celebration and Inspiration: Be a part of our uplifting community that celebrates milestones and embraces the joy of achievement.

Empowerment at Its Core: Empowerment isn't just a word; it's a way of life in the Rich Friends Circle. Embrace the mindset, money management, and mission that will lead you to abundance.

Are you ready to embrace the richness of life in every sense? If you're passionate about your growth and committed to creating a life of no regrets, the Rich Friends Circle is the perfect place for you.

Don't wait for another moment; your abundant life awaits!

Join the Rich Friends Circle now and be a part of this empowering journey!

Visit www.tmacinspired.com to claim your spot today!

Let's thrive together, one empowering step at a time!

With excitement and anticipation,

Dr. Tasha McCray

Founder of The Rich Friends Circle
Entrepreneur, Author, Investor, and Your Empowerment Advocate

Meet Dr. Tasha McCray

Dr. Tasha McCray is a true inspiration—an accomplished individual with a multifaceted background and an unyielding spirit. As a retired MSN-Ed, RN, and former hair stylist, she has excelled in various domains, including entrepreneurship, real estate investing, and authorship. But her path to triumph was paved with determination and resilience, overcoming the challenges of being a teenage parent at just thirteen years old. Fueled by her love for her son, she embarked on a relentless pursuit of creating a better life.

With a profound nursing career spanning 25 years, Tasha took a leap into the world of real estate as a private money lender. This pivotal step unlocked a passion for building her own portfolio using creative financing and unique strategies. Her business acumen revealed the importance of proper structures, unwavering commitment, and the power of working smarter, not harder.

Tasha's dedication extended beyond her personal success; she found her purpose in empowering fellow women entrepreneurs to elevate their businesses and financial status without sacrificing time and energy. Sharing her expertise and experiences, she taught them to establish proper systems for growth. After all, the quickest and most effective path to success is often guided by those who have walked a similar journey.

Fueling her passion for community building, Dr. Tasha McCray founded the "Rich Friends Circle" - a vibrant and supportive community for women entrepreneurs and professionals. This empowering circle fosters connections, collaboration, and mutual growth, uniting goal-oriented women on a mission to thrive and achieve their dreams together.

Over the last 5 years, Dr. Tasha McCray has witnessed her business skyrocket from six-figure years to 6-figure days, all while emphasizing the significance of mindset, money management, and purpose-driven missions. Her dedication to lifelong learning led her to receive an Honorary Doctorate of Philosophy in recognition of her 26+ years of contributions to the Entrepreneurship and Business Administration industry from Trinity Christian University's esteemed Business Honors Program. She also earned an Entrepreneurship Coach Certification, further empowering her to positively impact the nation.

Beyond her illustrious career, Tasha cherishes her blended family of 7 children and 6 grandchildren, who are her pride and joy. Together with her loving husband, Benny, she enjoys the simple joys of life, whether it's playing tennis, golfing, riding motorcycles, or embarking on memorable RV trips around the country.

Join Dr. Tasha McCray on an awe-inspiring journey through her book, where she shares her wisdom, lessons, and secrets to success. Embrace the mindset and strategies that have propelled her to remarkable heights. Prepare to be inspired, motivated, and ready to create your own rich life of abundance.

Made in the USA
Columbia, SC
27 October 2023

24670606R00091